MAN CREATED GOD!

No, Really, Why This Is Good News For All

ZBIGNIEW ALEXANDER

First Edition

PAGE PUBLISHING, INC.
New York, NY

First originally published by Page Publishing, Inc. 2016

ISBN 978-1-68289-438-5 (pbk)
ISBN 978-1-68289-439-2 (digital)

Printed in the United States of America

In any endeavor undertaken, humans crave support.
More so when ideology flirts with controversy.
This book was no exception but I received support in spades.
THANKS!
To my friends and extended family, you know who you are.
To my immediate family who never once discouraged me.
To my beloved wife, with your serenity I persevered,
and for this, my gratitude, for this, my love!

CONTENTS

PREFACE

It was at a New Year's dinner party at the start of this millennium, December 31, 1999, that I announced my intention to write a book. I did not describe the book, of course, for obvious reasons, the least of which was that religion is not a dinner conversation topic.

The idea had been kicking around in my head for years before that, fueled by the dismay with which I viewed the rise of religious fundamentalism in my country, the United States. Since the election of Ronald Reagan in 1980, the religious right had been pretty openly active and influential in American public life. This is not inherently bad if all it does is add to the tapestry of political pluralism in this country, but sadly, such was not the case. Far too often, when things go awry in a society, it takes a while for the masses to become actively involved in finding solutions. This creates a vacuum which is too easily filled by aggressive, extremist ideologies that had been waiting in the wings all along, building up a following, and biding their time. Ronald Reagan was a timely and perfect vehicle for unleashing this built-up potential after the disastrous economic, political, and "liberal" times of Jimmy Carter.

It is not that America suddenly found God. America had always harbored more religious fervor than Europe. This was, after all, one (though by no means all) of the reasons it came to be. Many of the earliest nonnative Americans were groups that were fleeing Europe to find a haven where they could practice their own particular religious beliefs with no impositions from others and without fear and hindrance—a religion more adaptive to the New World, at least in the North. In the Southern states, however, the denominations that evolved were more literal and biblical, restrictive rather than permissive. In fact, it is the opinion of this author that the whole of South America, by and large, did not experience the same direction of growth as North America partly because the same oppressive religious baggage prevailing back home came with the Spaniards, Inquisition included!

After the Civil War, and particularly in the last century, the formerly smaller Christian denominations in the South grew at a much faster rate than, and became increasingly farther removed from the older, established denominations of the North, and, with this growth, exerted more influence on the politics of the land. Religious institutions, particularly in the South, at first fell in line with Jim Crow politics, the American version of apartheid, and when this was finally outlawed in the last century by the civil rights legislation of the '60s, they quickly turned a new page and became the repository of "values," "morality," and the "American way"—the latter covering everything from capitalism to individualism. Those who did not share their values were labeled as un-American, Socialist, Communist, and so on.

It is this, more than anything else, that gets me. Long before Muslim extremists hijacked their religion, Christian extremists hijacked ours. It gets me that we see the damage resulting from the one but are blind to the consequences of the other. Consequences that affect the wars we wage, the way we view and treat our society, even the way we view and treat our planet. On top of all this, when I considered the fact that a personal God as defined by all these religions is an impossible hypothesis, the irony of it all screamed out to be heard. Enough, enough, enough! Let other voices be heard. Let the apathy of the masses be challenged. Let us stop and listen to alternative viewpoints.

You may note that this book is extremely slim. There are two reasons for this. First, I believe that what I have to say is best said succinctly and not belabored over and over in an interminable treatise. Second, and actually just as important for me, I believe brevity ought to be a goal for all authors today. For the past fifteen years or so, I have always maintained that any book today should not exceed 250 pages and should preferably be much shorter. In a world that is as highly connected and informed as we are today, there are just too many sources of information and entertainment available and demanding our attention. Books are now only one source of a great many where formerly they were one of very few media options. The average interested and informed person has access to Twitter, Facebook, the Internet, Webinars, tons of TV and cable programs, newspapers, magazines, and so on, and all of these or enough of them available instantly for download to his/her mobile device so as to stay always connected and informed no matter where they are or what they are doing or what day or hour it is. In such an environment, who has the time to read a one thousand-page volume? Is it not inconsiderate, if not arrogant, for an author to say in four hundred pages what could probably be stated just as effectively, if not more so, in two hundred?

In writing this book, I have availed myself of the many excellent books recently and not so recently published on this and related subjects. Here is a list of those I liked most, in no particular order, and I take this opportunity to thank the authors for their work which has informed and inspired this book: *The World's Religions* by Huston Smith; *American Theocracy* by Kevin Phillips; *The God Delusion* by Richard Dawkins; *God: The Failed Hypothesis* by Victor Stenger; *The End of Faith: Religion, Terror, and the Future of Reason* by Sam Harris; *God Is Not Great: How Religion Poisons Everything* by Christopher Hitchens.

I was fortunate to have been exposed to many, many faiths and cultures on three continents and in four countries. After earning a bachelor's degree in physics I spent my professional life in business. I researched this book from the data around us: written, broadcast, scientific and other articles, especially on the web—life experience! Despite the above exposure, I am particularly indebted to Sam Huston's *The World's Religions* for insights that I found invaluable and that I had missed despite my early exposure to those faiths and cultures.

I hope you find something here to stimulate awareness, discussion, and perspective. Revisiting our recent history from different (humanistic) angles has made me aware of the importance of looking behind the facade and the very real need to immediately start mapping out the world and society our grandchildren will inherit before others present us with a fait accompli of apocalyptic proportions.

On a more immediate and final note, I must beg for your patience and pardon for the liberties I have taken with the English grammar. I have used capital letters with abandon where I thought it necessary to enhance the meaning, emphasis, and nuance of words that denote a significant concept or play a primary role in my thesis. For instance, in the first chapter, second paragraph, the words GOD, CREATION, ORIGIN, and SCIENCE stand out and resonate not just when we first read them or meet those concepts, as it were, but with a resonance that lingers and is recalled whenever we read those same words again. Hopefully this will help you read the book exactly the way that I felt it and meant it.

CHAPTER 1

ORIGINS

> It is far better to grasp the Universe as it really is than to persist in delusion, however satisfying and reassuring.
>
> —Carl Sagan

This book is about GOD, RELIGION, and MAN—the part each played in human history, where each stands today, and what their future evolution could, indeed should, look like. Let me first clarify that the GOD I talk about is the very same God that most existing religions worship, particularly the "PERSONAL GOD" of Judaism, Christianity, and Islam. Though the latter religions refuse to admit it, this is the same God worshipped by Hindus, or maybe Buddhists, etc.

Since GOD is credited with having started it all by creating everything, I can't think of a better place to begin with than what is conventionally referred to as CREATION. However, permit me to immediately substitute ORIGIN for creation since creation implies there must be one or more creators, be they life-forms or not. I will simply limit myself to relate what SCIENCE currently tells us about the origin of our universe, the wonders of its beginning, its present, and its future. You decide whether a creator or creators are indispensable to this narrative or not. At the outset, I must state that it is perfectly true that the final chapters on our origins have yet to be written, particularly in regards to the very first instants as explained below. There are as yet no definitive answers. New theories and models are continually being put forward, and this is exactly what science is about—a constant updating of our ideas and knowledge, a filling in of gaps as new insight is obtained. But this state of evolution of knowledge, far from complete, should by no means be reason enough not to use and rely on current knowledge to develop the ideas addressed in this book because it is vastly more complete and accurate than the knowledge paradigms that preceded it. To my way of thinking, the actual way the universe came into existence is more breathtaking, more incredibly awesome than any version narrated in the "sacred" books.

The most widely held theory about the origin of our universe is the big bang. The astronomer, Fred Hoyle, first used the term *big bang* in a 1949 broadcast to distinguish between two theories of the origin of the universe. He is said to have used it derogatorily. Of the two prevailing theories at the time, he preferred the other—the constant state theory (no beginning or end).

One of the mysteries that confronted us when contemplating the universe was whether it had a beginning or had it always existed. That mystery has now been all but completely dispelled. By extrapolating backward in time, using general relativity, we find that our universe did indeed have a beginning in the distant past as an unimaginably small, extremely dense, extremely hot entity. Science has rigorously resolved most of the questions surrounding this scenario using standard methodology. First, a hypothesis is postulated and stated in precise mathematical terms. From this hypothesis, conclusions are drawn and predictions are made. Ideally, each part of the hypothesis from which an outcome can be predicted will have that outcome observed and confirmed. No need to go into the rigors of scientific method. You can rest assured, however, that when the majority of scientists begin to heavily favor one hypothesis over others, there is indeed a very good chance that it is the one that is truth, not fiction. When most major predictions of the theory have been confirmed by physical observations, you know you have a winner. This is the case with the big bang.

Most predictions of the big bang theory have been so confirmed. These include the following: (a) the existence of cosmic microwave background radiation, (b) the fact that CMBR was warmer in the past, (c) the universe is expanding at an increasing rate, (d) the universe is flattened and homogeneous, and (e) the timing of the creation of certain elements. The big bang theory has evolved to its current state as the result of 150 years of investigation and study by countless scientists—astronomers, cosmologists, physicists, and mathematicians.

The only part of the big bang hypothesis still up for grabs, so to speak, is the very first instant of emergence itself, the first 10^{-43} seconds, or the Planck Period, as it is called, and what the state was at that point, at the start of which even space and time did not exist.

For that matter, we have yet to venture beyond that point, if indeed there could be anything prior to it (the beginning), which I can only describe as "IRREALITY". You can see why scientists are having a devilish time with this. In other words, did the universe start as a SINGULARITY (see below)? Did it start as an even more exotic quantum entity, an INFLATON (my word, for want of a better one to describe the initial infinitely small, infinitely dense, infinitely hot, or approaching infinitely everything elementary particle soup) that experienced INFLATIONARY EXPANSION? Did it emerge from a STATE OF NOTHINGNESS (NON-SINGULAR?)? Or was something even more exotic, singular, and as yet beyond the grasp of our mathematics, our imaginations, and very likely, our comprehension involved?

One of the early proposals of the possible state of the universe at this period was a SINGULARITY—a single point of zero space and zero time (time and space came into existence later, instants after the big bang), but with infinite density and infinitely high temperature. At this point, all the known laws of physics, including general relativity, break down. Such a singularity is inherently unpredictable, and any configuration of outcomes is possible. It is the spontaneous, explosive resolution of this singularity and its immediate outcome into the expanding universe that is referred to as the big bang. This theory left us with several serious gaps in our understanding, particularly these three:

1. How did the universe become flat and homogeneous?
2. How do we explain the horizon problem? Distant objects in space are so far apart that the time for light to travel between them exceeds the age of the universe, yet their cosmic background radiation temperature indicates they were in contact in the past.
3. The monopole problem. Magnetic monopoles, if they indeed exist, are much rarer than the big bang theory predicts.

The INFLATIONARY EXPONENTIAL EXPANSION theory elegantly covers these gaps and provides a smooth transition through the very earliest instants of the emergence of the universe. Inflation has now been acknowledged as a more acceptable extension to the big bang. But not all the kinks have been ironed out here either. The jury is still out on this very earliest period of the universe. WHAT IS NO LONGER IN DOUBT THOUGH, IS THAT OUR UNIVERSE DID HAVE A BEGINNING—IT IS NOT ETERNAL—AND THIS HAPPENED A VERY LONG TIME AGO! A beginning, however, far removed from the intervention of a supernatural being with the characteristics of the personal God that appears in the religions of man, and far removed in time from the beginning dates postulated in religious texts.

So let us restate and be very clear about what happened all those eons ago. An unpredictable, random outcome from a primordial, infinitesimally small speck of infinite density, temperature, and pressure, gave birth to our universe some 13.7 billion years ago.. The very early history of the origin of our universe is an ongoing story as riveting as any ever told. Why, I started to write this book back in 2005. Now it is 2015, and as recently as July 4, 2012, the discovery of the God particle—the Higgs boson—was announced! This discovery is paramount, perhaps tantamount to the validity of the standard model, and scientists had been working on it for the past forty years. I feel confident that one day, most of the remaining speculation will be put to rest, and we will have an understanding of our origins as unshakable as we do of our own DNA. Not to confuse the situation, but the standard model, by the way, postulates that all matter and energy is derived from elementary particles which are several magnitudes smaller than atoms and come in several flavors, so to speak: some massless, others with mass; some with a positive charge, others negative, and yet others with no charge; some producing the gravitational force, others the weak force and others the strong force, and so on. Between them and their characteristics, elementary quantum physics has evolved to explain most everything at the subatomic scale. The major challenge facing physicists now is to tie the quantum physics universe with the Einsteinian universe explained by relativity.

At the risk of laboring a point, let us take a more detailed look at the generally accepted time line of our universe. It is important to dwell on this because it shows a completely natural, painstakingly long (by our sense of time), predictable, yet riddled-with-randomness progression from its primeval to its current state. While you read this, try and imagine an "intelligence" behind it all, and try and imagine at what stage the intelligence intervenes, if at all, and what kind of intelligence that would be. Would it be one that values humans above all else in the universe, long, long before humans arrived? Would it be one that intervenes in human affairs, favors one group over another, has prepared a heaven or a hell for us, and generally gives a damn? Repeat this exercise when you read the time lines of human evolution and human cultural evolution that follow. The stark truth is that, from the moment of the big bang, there is nothing, absolutely nothing, that has happened that cannot be explained as nature taking its course, or as the laws of physics that developed naturally from spontaneous events having sway. There is absolutely no reason to suppose that the universe would not have developed, as it did, without intelligent intervention.

Timeline of the Evolution of the Universe

The Very Early Universe

The very earliest life of the universe, the first 10^{-12} seconds, yes the first 0.000000000001 or one hundred billionth of a second, is the most speculative, since the known laws of physics cannot exist during this period and cannot provide the answers.

INFLATIONARY theory, or rather, the inflation paradigm, explains this initial phase, or most of it, rather admirably and elegantly. There are currently over fifty inflation theories proposed since Alan Guth first presented his in 1980. In the more accepted scenario, we start with a relatively very small field in the order of a billion times smaller than a single proton, where energies have so dramatically increased that gravity is reversed and becomes repulsive. This would have been the situation at close to time zero. At this point, exponential inflation occurs. According to elementary physics, this inflation occurs at a rate of doubling in size every 10^{-35} seconds. During this inflation, *density is preserved*, thus the original and relatively small but hugely dense mass of particles also increases exponentially. As this matter increases, the total positive energy grows, but so does the negative gravitational energy, helping to keep total energy in balance. Another feature of inflation is that the repulsive gravity material produced decays rapidly into particles of matter in the immediate post-inflationary stage, which occurs after about a hundred or so doublings, putting us at about 10^{-33} seconds into the big bang. We are left with a universe the size of a large marble—but hugely massive—containing a hot, dense, quark-gluon plasma. Now how does that grab you? To me it is far more dramatic than mythical stories about creation.

The Early Universe

From 10^{-12} seconds to ten seconds after the big bang, the hugely dense amount of matter and antimatter particles that was created during inflation results in mutual annihilation proceeding apace until the relatively small surviving excess of matter over antimatter is still large enough to give us all the building blocks from which the current universe was forged.

Starting around three minutes, protons and neutrons have formed and combine into atomic nuclei via nuclear fusion, and at around twenty minutes, temperature has cooled enough to stop this process, leaving three times more hydrogen nuclei than helium-4, and only trace amounts of other nuclei.

By seventy thousand years old, dark matter predominates. By 377,000 years, hydrogen and helium atoms begin to form, initially ionized, but quickly capturing electrons and becoming neutral. This allows the photons to travel freely, and this is what we observe as the cosmic microwave background noise.

Between 150 million to 1 billion years of age, the majestically large cosmological objects we are familiar with started appearing. First, quasars formed from intense gravitational collapse and reionized the universe with their intense radiation. Subsequently, the first population III or metal-free stars are formed and convert light elements into heavier ones. These stars were comparatively short-lived and ended in spectacular supernovae. From their debris, population II stars later evolved, producing more metal-enriched debris from their deaths.

Fast forward billions of years during which time vast clouds of dust and stellar debris form into galaxies in which new stars are born, die, and are reborn and all our heavy elements are forged.

Gravity pulls galaxies toward each other to form groups, clusters, and superclusters. The Milky Way galaxy was formed this way some 8.3 ± 1.8 billion years ago, and in these galaxies planets formed around some of the stars. Our sun is one such star in The Milky Way and our earth one such planet.

Let us pause now and take a closer look at our more immediate history (bya means billions of years ago and so on):

Time Line of the Earth's and Human Evolution

4.8 bya—The sun formed in the Milky Way
4.5 bya—The Earth formed
3.8 bya—We get simple cells (prokaryotes), LIFE BEGINS!
3 bya—Photosynthesis appeared
2 bya—Complex cells arise (eukaryotes)
1 bya—Multicellular life developed
600 mya—Simple animals appeared
570 mya—Arthropods appeared (ancestors of insects, arachnids, and crustaceans)
550 mya—Complex animals evolved
500 mya—Fish and proto-amphibians evolved
475 mya—Land plants evolved
400 mya—Insects and seeds evolved
360 mya—Amphibians arrived
300 mya—Reptiles evolved
200 mya—Mammals evolved
150 mya—Birds evolved
130 mya—Flowers evolved
65–80 mya—The first primates evolved from a group of small nocturnal and arboreal, insect-eating mammals called the Euarchonta.
65 mya—The non-avian dinosaurs died out.
25 mya—Apes or the species Hominoidea appeared.

7 mya—Hominina speciate from the ancestors of the chimpanzees. They cope with their new environment on the ground, as opposed to trees, by becoming bipedal, giving them greater visibility and freeing their forelimbs for food-gathering and using tools. Hominin brain development underwent a huge surge starting 5 million years ago.

2.5 mya—After thousands of animal species had evolved only to disappear by natural catastrophes and disasters, the genus HOMO appeared.
1.8 mya—*Homo erectus* appeared in Africa. Had a brain 74 percent the size of modern humans, migrates out of Africa and colonizes Eurasia.

516,000 years ago, *Homo antecessor,* the common ancestor of humans and Neanderthals, appeared.

200,000 years ago, *Homo sapiens* appeared and started to look like modern man.

160,000 years ago, *Homo sapiens* remains from this period were found in Ethiopia. They butchered hippos and practiced mortuary rituals.

150,000 years ago, mitochondrial Eve appeared in East Africa. She was the female ancestor common to all human mitochondrial lineages alive today.

100,000 years ago, *Homo sapiens* moved out of Africa to the Middle East.

60,000 years ago, man reached Australia, crossing the last sixty miles by boat. Y-chromosomal Adam lived in Africa (the most recent common ancestor from whom all human male Y chromosomes descended).

50,000 years ago, humans migrated out of Africa to South Asia.

40,000 years ago, man populated China and Asia.

30,000 years ago, human language is thought to have developed. By this time (thirty to fifty thousand years ago), modern behavior had evolved—figurative art, trade, music, burial rites, ornaments.

20,000 to 15,000 years ago, man arrived in the Americas crossing the Bering Strait by foot, and perhaps boating down the coast to avoid the Canadian ice sheet.

12,000 years ago, the evolution of light skin in Europeans occurred.

10,000 years ago, the Mesolithic period started. Fishing tackle, canoes, and bows appeared.

8,000 years ago, we were in the Neolithic period. Farming and the New Stone Age started.

5,000 years ago, proto-writing systems and the potter's wheel were invented.

4,000 years ago, we were in the Chalcolithic period. The copper age started with some iron use found.

3,500 years ago, the early Bronze Age started. The plow appeared.

3,000 to 2,000 years ago, urbanization, the first engineered roadway, sewage systems, sails, pottery, and writings on tablets appeared. Imperialism grew, and the Egyptian civilization peaked. Greco-Roman civilization developed. The major religions developed: Hinduism, Jainism, Buddhism, Judaism, Zoroastrianism. Literature developed in Greco-Roman Europe, India, and China. World population rose to 30 million.

2,000 to 1,000 years ago, the middle Bronze Age began. Christianity was founded, the Roman Empire fell, and in Europe, the late Bronze Age began and the Middle Ages started. Teotihuacan dominated Mesoamerica, and Japan embraced Buddhism and Confucianism, both of which contributed significantly to society in that country. ISLAM was founded by Muhammad. Paper, algebra, steel, and the magnetic compass were invented. The Iron Age started.

1,000 years ago to present, world population headed towards 50 million in the year 1,000CE. This millennium, particularly the last couple of centuries, saw the greatest explosion of science and technological advances the world has ever known. It started out ominously in the later Middle Ages. The NEW WORLD was discovered. Democracy established itself as the most promising form of organizing human society. The millennium ended, however, in a century that saw ethnic and racist prejudice, "informed" by religious/cultural intolerance, play a devastating role in the most horrific violence in human history—the Nazi-inspired Holocaust which massacred six million Jews. The last decade, the 1990s, saw more religious and sectarian violence and destruction in the Southeast European country of Bosnia-Herzegovina. The two world wars and other regional conflicts of the last century saw more people killed than all of the world's population a millennium ago. At the end of the millennium, however, population had increased to 6 billion.

Today, the first decade and a half of this new millennium will go down as one plagued by religious strife. The Islamic JIHADISTS seek to impose their harsh rule, employing terror directed indiscriminately and randomly against civilian populations. These jihadists have hijacked their religion, and in its name, are recruiting terrorists and suicide bombers. But whether openly sanctioned by the powers that be, as in the case of the past CRUSADES, or fanned by fanaticism and supported by rogue regimes and organizations, as in the case of the jihadists, religion, in my mind, far from promoting a progressive coming together which is what the world now needs, continues to bequeath a legacy of divisive harm.

I am not sure about you, but I am left breathless after viewing the absolutely awesome unfolding of our EVOLUTION and HISTORY. The endless series of twist and turns left a distinct impression of randomness, of trial and error, of spontaneity and sheer abundance—an abundance of options, an abundance of forms, an abundance of systems, an abundance of scale, an abundance of processes, and an abundance of outcomes.

It is almost like seeing one of the primary characteristics of the universe unfold before us—ENTROPY. From the "order" of the original miniscule inflation or singularity, to the vast expanse and complexity of our SPACE-TIME fabric, DISORDER is ever increasing.

So much for our ORIGIN and progress to date. Before proceeding to a discussion of the future, let me revisit the eternal question: "What was there before all of this, before the big bang?" I get heaped with ridicule when I reply that the actual state of the universe at the very instant of origin is frankly unknown, but in all probability, there was *nothing* before it, and in some yet-to-be-discovered way, the universe arose out of nothing. It is at this point that people seem to want to scream, "It's the Creator, dummy, don't you see this?" I really don't! If you follow this line of reasoning, then who created the Creator? Don't *you* see? "Well," you say, "the Creator is eternal, he always was, and always will be." An elegant hypothesis, I'll admit, but quite illogical and equally preposterous. If there could be one being who is eternal, why cannot there be others, each separate, and, by definition, independent of the other? And why, indeed, must eternity be confined to a living entity, why not inanimate matter? That very special something that had to exist eternally before the universe did, why could it not be INANIMATE and UNINTELLIGENT? If something is eternal and is not created, surely it is just as likely to be inanimate and unintelligent as living and intelligent. After all, it *was never brought into or came into* existence, it just always was, totally independent of all else. Saying that ultimately only the intelligent creator always was and always will be, is, in fact, more absurd than the hypotheses science has postulated, because there are mathematical models that set out to prove, test, and validate the scientific hypotheses, including the one that there was probably nothing before the big bang, whereas creationism's creator simply has to be eternal for it to work! Simple and elegant, maybe—feeble, definitely!

The Future of the Universe

Predicting the future of the universe is even more difficult than determining our past. There are observable results of what happened in the past that allow hypotheses to be confirmed with substantial confidence. No such privileged observations and information exist for the future, for the obvious reason that it has not happened yet.

Theories, however, can and are developed with gusto as the future is as fascinating a subject as our past. For the time being, however, they remain theories. Suffice it to say that the various outcomes are all rather inglorious such as (a) the BIG RIP with the universe expanding at ever increasing rates till it is torn asunder even at the atomic and subatomic levels; (b) the BIG FREEZE, currently the most widely held theory, where the universe expands at more modest rates and its temperature approaches absolute zero, ending as a sparse, almost empty, cold and dark collection of black holes and little else; or (c) the BIG CRUNCH, where the expansion is eventually stopped and contraction begins with unknown results—among which exists the possibility of the universe falling back on itself till it is compressed into a singularity once more and possibly emerges as another universe through another BIG BANG, though this scenario is thought to be less likely. Other more exotic speculation exists, and it will be a while before the science is there to give us a more thoroughly reasoned and confident answer.

The science of the origin and fate of the universe is still very much alive and evolving. There is still a great deal to be learned. One thing, however, is clear to the vast majority of scientists who have worked in this field over the last 250 years or so: the fundamental laws of nature, including those of mathematics and physics, are all that are needed to explain the universe—laws that themselves do not require supernatural intervention to exist. Where there are gaps in our knowledge or a lack of overwhelming scientific agreement on an issue, as in our theories about the very instant of the appearance of the universe, there is every confidence that it is merely a matter of time before a fuller understanding will emerge. Science is like this.

It is a gradual progression from a lesser to a fuller understanding of nature. My only request to you, dear reader, would be to always keep in mind these two considerations: the enormous time scale, billions of years, on the one hand, and the enormous unpredictability and randomness on the other. *This is how we got here*!

Conclusion

Against this backdrop, any talk of a CREATOR having done all this just so he could create us, MAN, is absurd in the highest degree, at least to my way of thinking. The most obvious conclusion would be that such a creator, if he existed, must have been unable to get it right the first time. Countless species had to emerge and disappear, and countless versions of *Homo* tossed into the scrap heap of evolution until the final, far-from-perfect model was settled on. In fact, *are* we the final outcome, or are there other installments of the saga due? Is this the work of an OMNIPOTENT, OMNISCIENT, COMPASSIONATE being? Hardly! Possibly, too, the same "experiment" was performed at countless times in countless other worlds with varying degrees of success. Success, truth be told, that is entirely in the eye of the beholder.

If there is intelligence behind all of this, it is more like the work of a (MAD) SCIENTIST or a group of them or a very IMPERSONAL (INANIMATE?) GOD or an eternally preexisting inanimate entity. Perhaps a runaway project in another universe that has had unpredictable results. Or, as many scientists believed, indeed the majority, not so much the result of INTELLIGENT DESIGN but of SPONTANEOUS NATURAL PHENOMENA. No matter how I look at it from the perspective science gives us, I see no reason whatsoever to imagine a personal God like the God of Abraham or Lord Shiva or Allah who listens to our prayers, communicates with us, intervenes in our affairs, and, while at it, pits one faction against another.

I will not spend any more time reasoning that GOD, *as defined by most religions,* simply does not exist. Let me refer you to more exhaustive, eloquent, and rigorous expositions of the topic. One book that I particularly like is *God: The Failed Hypothesis* by Victor J. Stenger, where he focuses exclusively on the attributes of the Judeo-Christian and Muslim God and methodically demonstrates that no observed evidence of such attributes can be found in the physical universe around us, hence such a God must not exist. For the sheer wonder of our universe, I recommend Brian Greene's *The Fabric of the Cosmos.* Another book worth reading is *The God Delusion* by Richard Dawkins, a renowned evolutionary scientist and ATHEIST, where he takes on the creationists and exquisitely presents the case for EVOLUTION; or you may try his *The Greatest Show on Earth: The Evidence for Evolution,* a spellbinding chronicle of evolution. There are many more, but I don't want to overload you and myself. Though quite enthralling, let's face it: some of this reading, not all, is quite heavy going.

Before leaving this chapter, let me offer a restatement of my thoughts on one of the major discussion points in any conversation on the origin of the universe: the notion that every effect must have a cause. This simple notion, it is argued, leads us to conclude that if anything exists, it must have been caused to exist, and this in turn leads us to believe that at some point in the past, our universe came into existence in its primordial form as the work of an entity who has no beginning, no cause, and is eternal. From its eternal nature, it follows (does it really?) that such an entity must have all the other various attributes that we ascribe to it such as oneness, intelligence, omnipotence, etc.

This argument rather inelegantly addresses the unanswerable question of what caused the beginning to begin. The fallacy, however, is that the eternal being argument is itself an illogical proposition. We are in fact saying that, OK, there absolutely has to be a cause for every effect except when there isn't—that at some point, we have an effect without a cause, and that this is GOD. As pointed out earlier, if indeed an entity could exist that is eternal, with no beginning and no end, why cannot there be more than one such being? Why, there may even be an infinite number of them! If GOD is eternal, he obviously did not create himself, and if this is possible, there clearly could be more beings like him who neither were created nor created themselves. And are they necessarily as intelligent and awesome as all that? Are they necessarily even "living beings"? If nothing is required to create them, why can they not be inanimate? The possibilities, as Margaret Thatcher used to say, are endless!

It is much wiser to admit that while we have made enormous progress in understanding our origins all the way back through 13.7 billion years, there are still some gaps and discussion points along the way; and before the first appearance of the universe, there is really only speculation. We can also say with confidence that just as we have ruled out the various gods we have worshiped in the storied past of our species, our current knowledge in no way leads us to suppose that before the point of the origin of the universe, there always was the personal GOD that we currently worship. If anything, the opposite is true, that if it is remotely possible (remoteness twice removed) that such a being exists, it is far from clear that it resembles our current notions of GOD! Any way you cut it, we do not have the slightest reason to believe that such a GOD exists, but every reason to believe that he does not.

Richard Dawkins said it best: "The universe we observe has precisely the properties we should expect if there is, at bottom, no design, no purpose, no evil, no good, nothing but blind, pitiless indifference."

All I wanted to accomplish in this chapter is to have my readers get a feel for where we stand in our current understanding of the universe—how and when it came into existence, how and when we came into being, and how and when it will all end. I believe that just by understanding the *scale* and *randomness* of it all, we have no alternative but to reject the notions of a personal God that have been instilled into us from our earliest consciousness, and *at the very least*, if intelligence is all we will accept, we begin to think, instead, of a detached and utterly *impersonal* intelligence. The next chapter, then, if God never did exist, will deal with how and when current notions of God came about.

End Notes

Much of the information in the time lines is available in various articles on the web that I accessed and organized to present a more concise and complete picture. Not all sources give the same dates but they are within what I would call acceptable variation.

CHAPTER 2

MAN CREATED GOD

> We are all atheists about most of the gods that humanity has ever believed in. Some of us just go one god further.
>
> —Richard Dawkins

A prerequisite for *creating* anything is INTELLIGENCE. "Aha!" you might say, "gotcha! You admit that creation requires intelligence, so you must admit the universe and life were created by intelligence." Nothing of the sort! At the start of the first chapter, I immediately replaced the word creation with origin. Creation presupposes intelligence, at least the way it is used in discussing the lofty subjects we do here, whereas origin does not presuppose anything. In this chapter, allow me to immediately distinguish not just between creation and origin, but between creation and evolution. Creation springs from intelligence, and evolution springs from a series of natural processes. Creation is deliberate and inherently controllable, while evolution is blind and inherently unstoppable. Science has clearly established the latter in the case of the lifeforms inhabiting our planet. It has also clearly explained the natural evolution of the universe from the big bang forward. Creation is this book you are reading or the dam a beaver builds across a stream. Evolution is the beaver being a far removed cousin of yours (and mine). It is also the dam-building beaver being "selected" for survival, and his dam-less brothers facing, well, damnation. Evolution endowed life-forms with varying degrees of intelligence. Man happens to have the highest form of intelligence we are aware of. Let us briefly see how this may have developed and what the consequences were.

During the course of the earth's history, ice ages have come and gone, and they have played a very important role in geology, climate, and the evolution of life. As a matter of fact, we are currently *in* an ice age, the Pliocene-Quaternary glaciation which started 2.58 million years ago! There have been at least five major ice ages starting about 2.1 billion years ago, each lasting several millions of years.

About 7 million years ago, as mentioned in chapter 1, "Time Line of the Earth's and Human Evolution," tree-dwelling animals were forced into the open grasslands which replaced continuous forests in significant areas as a result of an ice age. These animals adapted to their new environment by becoming bipedal and walking on their hind legs. Over time, prodigious evolutionary changes occurred, like those that provided greater elevation of their eyes for protection, and forelimbs that could be used for gathering food and using simple tools. Most importantly, the brain size increased dramatically, partly to drive these capabilities and to assure the survival of their species. No, let me rephrase that: evolution assured the natural selection of the brainier ones for future generations as these were the ones with the higher survival rate. It is, thus, a few million years later, that the hominid species appeared.

The increased brain size in turn, in man's early manifestations, made it necessary for birth to take place sooner than ideally would be the case while the birth canal was sufficiently wide for the larger skull, yet not so wide that it compromised the female's level of mobility. The offspring of this species, less than ideally developed (as far as the brain is concerned) at the time of birth in order to meet these size restrictions, thus required a longer, more intensive, child-rearing period. A more intensive rearing period which, by the way, was inevitable because the larger brain came with just the necessary hardwiring and was always "evolved" for considerable soft programming.

It was true back then and it is true today, that the "intelligent" brain is born with just the basic autonomous and instinctual functions hardwired. The remaining skills must always be acquired after birth and take years to instill. To accomplish this task, more social lifestyles were required from its members, and this led to living in groups and staying longer in their settlements. Longer stays in the same place required more dependence on food gathering which spurred more intensive tool use and organizational skills that further increased demands on brainpower.

The stage was set for the emergence of *Homo sapiens.* As an aside, let me state that during this phase of evolution, we also see what I consider to be another evolutionary principle in play, and you scientists out there will forgive my frivolity—the principle of "If you don't use it, you lose it." Let us remember that our very close cousins, the apes, were also exposed to similar forces and also being endowed with larger brains, and God knows how many other close cousin branches out there in the savannas failed to capitalize and perished. They did not fully use it! It is felt that their innate aggression and competitiveness could have prevented them from making full use of this gift in the social, cooperative setting we have described. Who knows, perhaps other physiological traits came into play and restricted their further brain development.

It is my contention that this earlier birthing/longer rearing played a secondary but significant role in the development of brain size and intelligence. The longer the fetus is in the womb, the more Mother Nature can control and manage its development, the more "hardwiring" of its brain can be accomplished prior to birth and the less soft programming required once born. We are fortunate this was not the case, that the considerable soft programming possible after birth was facilitated by, and in turn facilitated more gray matter to be provided before birth. With everything hardwired, we probably would have been just other, albeit smarter, apes. There would be no need or possibility for innovative and creative thinking and experimenting. Of course there is also the possibility that that structure and functioning of the human brain that requires most learning to be soft programmed was "selected" as the most adaptable/survivable.

But back to our story. The earlier the birth, the less of a role played by hardwired instinct, and the more post-birth instruction, care, and protection required. Therefore, the more intelligence required from the parent(s) who now have to help provide some of the "programming" of the brain's hardware, as it were. In other words, the more adaptable the species! From this point on, brain development becomes a victim of its success, which is exactly what evolution is good at and all about—building on success! NATURAL SELECTION!

Concurrently with these developmental challenges of caring for the infant, competition from other social groups and individuals within groups becomes a driver requiring intelligent strategies and negotiating, social, communication, and other skills. Intelligence even became a factor in sexual selection. All of which ensured the brain's evolution to its current state. As with all things evolutionary, change did not come overnight. It was slow and imperceptible by human timescales—taking tens, perhaps hundreds of thousands of years, yet it was utterly relentless. And as with all things evolutionary, probably none of this would have happened if other species of predator-competitors, the dinosaurs et al., had not been removed fortuitously by an asteroid strike! Who knows what direction life-forms would have taken otherwise?

As we saw in the last chapter, we were not shaped, created, and then placed here in our existing state as a finished product by the Almighty. Not as a group nor as a single human from whom all others descended, nor in any of the fantastic ways suggested by creationists of all stripes. This is what most religions suggest. Instead, WE EVOLVED NATURALLY, THOUGH VERY ACCIDENTALLY, OVER MILLIONS OF YEARS—just like every other species of living creature around us did! We gradually discovered or became aware of our intelligence and free will and slowly and painstakingly learned how to use them. Evolution played its role here just as in every other facet of our lives, ensuring by selection, among other things, that those who made better use of these gifts survived and reproduced. Most sobering of all is that any one of a number of events could have resulted in alternative outcomes, and indeed, did, for countless species. Any of a number of events could have led to our extinction and may still do.

Finally, 13.7 billion years after the origin of the universe, 3.8 billion years after life first appeared on Earth, 5 million years after hominids separated from the last of their primate cousins, the chimpanzees, after a number of these related HOMO species had become or were soon to become extinct, *Homo sapiens* appeared some two hundred thousand years ago. He already possessed intelligence, and as we shall see below, he had a rudimentary language and ALREADY HAD RELIGION! It is conceivable that in the not too distant future, man will continue to develop and use his intelligence, and make every effort to influence evolution and take his species to levels unimaginable today.

In evolutionary terms, man descended from the HOMINA SPECIES. Along the way, HOMO ERGASTER (1.9 to 1.4 million years ago) is considered to be the first to develop language, and HOMO HEIDELBERGENSIS (600 to 350 thousand years ago) is considered to be the first to have religion, judging from burial practices, an indicator of religious beliefs, as we shall see later.

Yes, human language too owes its existence to evolution. It would not be possible without the large brain we have and without the physical attributes required to produce the multitude of sounds used in language—the principal one being the descended larynx. The human larynx is found much lower in the vocal tract than other primates, enabling complex sound production. If you consider the evolution described so far, it is not difficult to see how the need to communicate more effectively than just by a few sounds and signs became paramount when intelligence became such a significant factor in survival. Language, in fact, could have developed as early as 7 million years ago, when the physical attributes were in place in our ancestors, and no later than thirty-five thousand years ago, the date of cave art by Cro-Magnons, discovered in Europe, which indicate the existence of language and abstract thought.

It is likely, however, that real language skills developed around two hundred thousand years ago with the emergence of *Homo sapiens,* and either gradually improved over the ages or experienced a sudden spurt about thirty-five thousand years ago to relatively modern features.

Whatever the time line, language has been around far longer than recorded history. The oldest WRITING systems, however, are currently held to be the Sumerian cuneiform script (circa 3,400 BC or 5,400 years ago) and Egyptian hieroglyphs (3,200 BC or 5,200 years ago).

So we have a period, enormously long by the time line of our species, from tens of thousands to millions of years between the emergence of intelligence and language on the one hand, and written communication on the other; and between the emergence of inquiring minds to foster speculation on the one hand, and the writing tools to organize and handle such speculation on the other—eons of time in which to wreak a lot of mischief. IT WAS DURING THIS PERIOD THAT RELIGION EMERGED AND ESTABLISHED ITSELF FIRMLY IN OUR PSYCHE. It did not just arise in isolation, but wherever intelligence existed, patterns of beliefs and practices arose that were the earliest forms of religion.

These intelligent species, including *Homo sapiens,* as they evolved, became ever more "CONSCIOUS," that is, more aware of feelings, emotions, and abstractions. They identified the concepts of good and evil, of love and hatred, of courage and cowardice.

More so then, in those primitive times, than now, there were more questions than answers, and there was far more to be concerned about and little to allay those concerns. Disaster could come at any time from anywhere. When it did, because they were intelligent beings, they would search for, but not always find, a cause and effect explanation. Like thinking men, then as now, they felt compelled to formulate a hypothesis to explain everything. Even today, you can get an idea of that innate inquisitiveness from the thinking mind of a child. As soon as it learns how to speak (probably before that too, except we do not understand its "infant speak," and it certainly does not understand ours), it is full of questions asking why this, why that, why, why, why. Our first thinking ancestors often did come up with explanations for observed phenomena employing simple cause and effect reasoning. This helped them acquire hunting, gathering, child-rearing, toolmaking, and other skills. When the phenomena could not be explained by their primitive analytical skills, it was probably ignored, if insignificant, or if it was indeed significant, they ascribed it to an UNKNOWN or SUPERNATURAL origin. Again, where an effect was seen to exist but no cause or means creating the effect could be observed by the five senses, a SUPERNATURAL origin was presumed. In those settings, this was quite logical. Faith and dogma filled the void left by ignorance.

Intelligence is by its nature inclined to first observe and identify patterns of, say, repeated natural occurrences around it, and then assume a similar intelligence behind them absent other explanations. In those early eons, advanced scientific inquiry was totally absent. Thus, over the ages, the repeated rising and setting of the sun, the waxing and waning periods of the moon, the placement of the stars in the night sky, the changes of the seasons, the seasonal rain, thunder, and lightning—they were all found to be so remarkably predictable that they were ascribed to the intervention of intelligent beings, obviously very significant beings. It was not long before the sun and the moon themselves were deemed to be GODS.

Evolution had provided us with intelligence and emotions for our survival. Products of these attributes were our ability to discern and define good and evil, feel love and hatred, and distinguish right from wrong. All of this equipped us for survival. It was not long before disasters were ascribed to evil spirits, or to gods venting their wrath for wrongdoings. Yes, gods, too, were assigned the same attributes we possessed. It was not long before efforts were being made to placate those gods to avoid disasters. And it was not long before rivalry between one group's gods and another's played itself out in real life, on the battlefield.

RELIGION WAS BORN. MAN HAD CREATED GOD! HE DID SO IN HIS OWN IMAGE, WITH HIS OWN ATTRIBUTES, RAISED TO A MUCH HIGHER POWER. And he has never been able to deconstruct God since, to take back the control over his destiny that he gave up to these gods! It was a foregone conclusion that since the gods were endowed with all these powers, and they lived in another world at a higher level of existence, they would reward humans, their most favored creatures, by taking them to their abode if their life had pleased them, or banishing them to another world if not. Death was transformed from the natural phenomenon it really is for all species to a major transitional and transformational phase in man's existence. Burial became ritualistic both as forms of reverence for the deceased and as acknowledgment of the belief systems, including transition to other worlds, to an afterlife.

Populations became organized into larger social groups, dwelling in larger villages, and relations between groups of villages in geographically distinct spaces eventually lead to the formation of "nations" or "peoples." This led to a need for a more established and organized set of religious beliefs and practices. As stated above, burial practices were among the earliest that resulted from, or were associated with what we could call "religious" sentiment for their association with belief in afterlife. It is no stretch of the imagination that burials became an important part of the earliest organized religions, and the persons who performed the ceremonial burial rituals were the first priests, shamans, swamis, medicine men, etc.

From the very beginning, all of man's understanding of his environment fell into two categories: the natural and the supernatural. Naturally a far greater part of the universe, if not most of it, was initially incomprehensible to him. His initial understanding of the workings of the universe was limited to those aspects he could physically verify in a cause-effect manner. The supernatural thus played a great role in his life, certainly much greater than today.

Even after the development of writing systems, when knowledge and inquiry (learning) received a monumental surge, there was still a vast inventory of experience that was relegated to the mystical or supernatural. Long after man had learned farming, agriculture, metal working, and pottery, to name a few relatively modern skills, such events as storms and floods were attributed to the gods, and religions the world over required offerings and prayers to placate them and secure favorable outcomes. Even today, these practices persist. In 2011, Governor Perry of Texas designated Friday, April 22, through Sunday, April 24, as days of prayer for rain to alleviate the severe drought that Texas was suffering. Similar events have occurred in other parts of the United States. [2.1]

It was obvious that by its very nature, by definition, if you will, religion was not something you could prove, indeed it was everything that was not provable. Religion forced itself on people by requiring belief and blind faith. In any collection of individuals forced to live in groups, there is a natural and instinctive urge for some to rise to leadership positions. Where the species is also endowed with intelligence and FREE WILL, this becomes a very political process. Once religion became organized, it was not long before some priests became "high priests" and wielded considerable power—power which they had to learn to share with those other individuals who wielded the secular power: the tribal chiefs, lords, and kings. It was even inevitable that in some societies, the two functions were merged in the same individual, resulting in the god-kings of many primitive and not so primitive cultures (Japan's emperor, was considered to be divine, and the Dalai Lama too), and where this was not possible, resulting in the king usurping the position of high priest as Henry VIII did, to name just one, when he assumed the position of supreme head of the Church of England! Along the way you had the holy men, most of whom, but unfortunately not all of them, were genuinely so, men who dedicated themselves to religion and a life of service to their God and their fellow believers.

Religion thus got to play a role as vital, if not more so, as any other discipline in society and elicited intense fervor and devotion from the faithful. IT WAS A PERFECT FIT. Since man himself had created God, he could identify with all the divine attributes which were, after all, the same attributes that man himself had or wished he had but to a higher degree. Whether it was LOVE, MERCY, KNOWLEDGE, and FREE WILL, or POWER, WRATH, and RETRIBUTION—EVERY DIVINE ATTRIBUTE OF GOD WAS SOMETHING MAN HIMSELF WAS CAPABLE OF OR WISHED HE WAS. Man could thus identify, he could relate, and he could lose himself in his devotion to such a being. Such was the intensity of commitment of some of the faithful that they imagined themselves conversing with the divine—a phenomenon that modern medicine can account for in any of several ways which I shall not go into here. They became the recipients of direct revelation from the divine, and these revelations served to strengthen the religion, particularly when they came from the religious hierarchy supported by the secular power. These revelations were preserved and transmitted from generation to generation by religious ceremonies, chants, stories, paintings, and when writing developed, by written SCRIPTURE.

It does not matter in which age or part of the world you investigate religion, you will always find the same—at some point, God communicates or "reveals" himself to man. In many cases, these "revelations" become the scripture of the religion on which its dogma is based. In other instances, particularly where the religious and secular powers are not themselves the blessed recipients, or where the revelation is not of their liking, a heresy is declared, and the guilty one subjected to a summary hearing, excommunicated, or as often was the case in the past, put to death.

Not only has religion been a perfect fit for man's nature, but it has also been structured perfectly to resist attempts to dethrone it. How can you disprove that which is not provable in the first place? How can you challenge a person's beliefs when he starts by telling you those are not beliefs based on science or logic but pure "faith"? How can you easily purge those beliefs programmed into your brain since childhood? It does not matter what arguments you provide, and I will not go into any. Towards the end of the preface I already referred you to those who have done this far more eloquently than I can. Suffice it to say that faith endures, and even to this day, people swear as to the efficacy of their prayers. They say that God talks to them and intervenes in their lives. They continue to be devout and even fanatical in their beliefs. They often perform much good, but they often also cause much evil in the name of their God and their religion. Not just ordinary people—people with considerable power and ability to influence human affairs. And they program their children with their system of beliefs.

In December 1992, the first President George H. W. Bush, in an exhortation to the troops on their mission to Somalia, said this: "And so, to every sailor, soldier, airman and marine who is involved in this mission, let me say you're doing God's work."[(2.2)] His son, President George W. Bush, is reported to have felt very strongly that he was doing God's work in his wars against terror. Christian author, Stephen Mansfield, in his book *The Faith of George W. Bush,* relates what Bush commented to Texan evangelist Robinson, "I feel like God wants me to run for President. I can't explain it, but I sense my country is going to need me. Something is going to happen... I know it won't be easy on me or my family, but God wants me to do it."[(2.3)]

It is no secret that throughout human history there has been little separation between church and state. It is only in modern democracies that such a separation is supposed to exist. No wonder, then, that throughout history, leaders have hijacked religion to support their actions, or worse still, religion has hijacked leaders to impose its own designs. The untold destruction, misery, and suffering that has resulted is unimaginable.

End Notes

(2.1) abcnews.com, 4-21-2011, Texas Governor Urges Prayers For Rain
http://www.nbcnews.com/id/42705038/ns/weather/t/texas-governor-urges-rain-prayers-wildfire-battles-continue/

(2.2) NYTimes.COM; MISSION TO SOMALIA; Transcript of President's Address on Somalia
Published: December 5, 1992
http://www.nytimes.com/1992/12/05/world/mission-to-somalia-transcript-of-president-s-address-on-somalia.html

(2.3) Bush Says God Chose Him To Lead The Nation; Sunday, Novenber 2, 2003 http://www.theguardian.com/world/2003/nov/02/usa.religion

CHAPTER 3

MORALITY

> The following proposition seems to me in a high degree probable—namely, that any animal whatever, endowed with well-marked social instincts, the parental and filial affections being here included, would inevitably acquire a moral sense or conscience, as soon as its intellectual powers had become as well, or nearly as well developed, as in man. For, firstly, the social instincts lead an animal to take pleasure in the society of its fellows, to feel a certain amount of sympathy with them, and to perform various services for them.
>
> —Charles Darwin

If I had the time and the means, I would love to draw up a balance sheet of religion—on one side, all the GOOD that resulted from it, and on the other, all the EVIL. Yes, let there be no doubt that both results have accrued over the millennia. But I will leave this for a more intrepid soul.

Let me just turn to one of the most frequently cited contributions of religion—MORALITY, which, incidentally, is one of the most frequently cited casualties of the absence of religion. Well, surprise, surprise! RELIGION DID NOT GIVE US OUR MORALITY. Man's own evolution, over time, yielded the general precepts by which his species should abide to ensure survival. Aided by his unique ability for abstract thought, morality was bound to develop, just as surely as man's other traits and skills did. It has been argued that morality actually preceded religion, or at the very least, evolved together with it. Pre-moral behavior is even seen in primates and other species that live in groups—some, in fact, where the group is more significant and takes precedence over the individual, such as ants. I say this, of course, because morality is most meaningful, perhaps only meaningful, in the group context. Morality is, even today, more applicable to man's dealings with others than just in regard to his own person. Indeed, morality even covers man's dealings with his environment, including the whole spectrum of flora and fauna. The degree to which morality developed was governed, not by God, but entirely by the free will and intelligence that evolved in man. MORALITY WAS AN INEVITABLE PRODUCT OF EVOLUTION.

Today, and for thousands of years past, all societies exhibit similar basic moral codes irrespective of their particular religions. The Ten Commandments, currently so controversial in the judicial landscape of this country because displaying them in public buildings is seen as a violation of the separation between church and state, are not at all unique to Christendom or Judaism. I am not saying that other religions have the same ten commandments, but the same moral precepts are found not only in the Old Testament, but even earlier in India and China, and, I would venture to add, in all other parts of the world, independently of each other, and in all likelihood, quite SPONTANEOUSLY. A great example, often used in these discussions, is the GOLDEN RULE—to do to others as you would have them do to you. This not only appears in the Christian and Jewish faiths, but also in Islam and in ancient Egypt, China, India, Greece, and so on. To hear Christian preachers, one would think that humanity owes these moral codes of conduct exclusively to the Judeo-Christian tradition.

Let us take a look at the Golden Rule as we find it expressed through history:

Ancient Egypt, Middle Kingdom, 2040 to 1650 BCE: Now this is the command: Do to the doer to cause that he do.

Ancient Egypt, Late Period. 1080 to 332 BCE: That which you hate to be done to you, do not do to another.

Ancient Greece, attributed to Pittacus, 640–568 BCE: Do not to your neighbor what you would take ill from him.

Hinduism (Mahabharata, thought to have been composed between 600 and 400 BCE): One should never do that to another what one regards as injurious to one's own self. This, in brief, is the rule of dharma. Other behavior is due to selfish desires.

Judaism (Pentateuch, Leviticus 19:18, said to have been composed between 550 to 400 BCE): You shall not take vengeance or bear a grudge against your kinsfolk. Love your neighbor as yourself.

Confucius (Confucius lived from 551 to 479 BCE): Never impose on others what you would not choose for yourself.

Islam (Muhammad lived from 570 to 632 CE): Hurt no one so that no one may hurt you.

Which brings me to another point. Having satisfied myself that God, *as our religions define him*, simply does not exist, I find it amusing and at the same time highly irritating to see how we, in the Western world, when we talk of religion, we talk mostly of Christianity and Judaism. The Muslim faith is discussed today only in a dismissive way, increasingly in relation to TERRORISM, and the other major faiths, Buddhism and Hinduism, to mention just two, are largely ignored. When morality is discussed, it would appear that these other faiths do not have any, because they are never quoted or in any way embraced in the discussions. And this is done not only by religious figures, but by learned, secular authors. How arrogant!

How typical! Typical of each religion to see itself as superior! How selfish and how perpetuating of ignorance.

This is one reason I feel that often, the very good that religion does eventually devolves into evil, and let there be no doubt that over the years and centuries, it has done a tremendous amount of good (promoting and upholding—though not inventing—morality, science and education, compassionate ministering, patronizing the arts and science, exhorting peace and justice, and on and on). Unfortunately, the good actions undertaken under the auspices of religious institutions, more so in the past, almost always come with baggage, either in the form of indoctrination and conversion, or a total disregard of a population's own indigenous religion and customs. RELIGION BLINDS US TO ALL BUT OUR OWN BELIEFS AND DIRE ARE THE CONSEQUENCES! We see this clearly today in the situation in the Middle East, and let me take some time here to explain that situation at length from a GODLESS perspective.

Simply put, you have a group of people, the Jews, who, ages ago, believed (and still do) that their God had actually led them to and given them their land, the land he had promised them. Much later, some two thousand years ago, in 70 CE, they lost this land irretrievably when Rome finally crushed a Jewish revolt, destroying the Second Temple in Jerusalem in the process. Since then, they had been settling wherever they could, mostly in Europe, east and west. For reasons also connected with belief in God (both theirs and others'), they were horribly victimized over the centuries, and, not surprisingly, never forgot their "promised" land and yearned to return to it.

Meanwhile, they survived by often doing what the people of their host societies, their oppressors, would not do—most pertinent to our case: lending money (considered sinful by some of the non-Jewish faiths), administration of public and private organizations (the local gentry preferred to be gentleman landowners and farmers rather than administrators), and other professional services (medicine, sciences, etc., also unappealing to the local populations). Because of this, the Jews acquired great knowledge and skills in all the aforementioned fields. They also accumulated great wealth and power despite the fact that they were a much maligned and victimized group. They were then, and are now, indeed, a people worthy of our utmost admiration—a perfect example of the survival instinct of the human race as individuals and as groups. I am hard-pressed to find another group that so doggedly preserved their culture and traditions against all odds.

In hindsight, this was the only successful strategy they could have used. Being rejected from mainstream society in practically all the countries they sought out, they survived by occupying indispensable and essential niches in those same societies while at the same time steadfastly maintaining their cultural and religious identity as a people, often in forced segregation. Wherever and whenever possible, they would also integrate themselves into their new cultural environment like any other people through the ages.

By the latter part of the nineteenth century, it was no wonder that the tragedy of their situation had intensified over the centuries to such an extent that it stirred the Jews' yearning to return to their homeland and found expression in the Zionist movement.

Later, during the First World War, when Britain was brought to its knees and was faced with the imminent threat of failure and defeat if it could not find the funds to finance its war effort, it turned to the powerful and influential Jewish financial community, and, to make a long story short, was given the money it sought in return for a resolution by the British cabinet stating that a return to the homeland (Palestine) by the Jews would not be opposed. As the appointed "administrator" of Palestine, Britain obviously assumed it had the jurisdiction to do this.

With the resulting Balfour Declaration (look it up, try *Wikipedia,* fascinating reading) that acknowledged and sanctioned this policy, the exodus began, and what had been a trickle of Jewish immigrants to Palestine became a veritable flood. The people living in Palestine at the time were mostly Muslims, and some could trace their roots there eight hundred years back or so. Naturally, they became increasingly alarmed and protested loud and clear, of course, but to no avail. They never had a chance, not then, and much less later, as we shall see.

Right from the beginning, there were clashes. Why are these people coming to our land to settle permanently, with the idea of carving out their own state? On whose authority? What about our rights derived from living here for generations upon generations over some eight hundred years? Just as the tension and conflict grew ever more tense, World War II broke out, and when it ended, the world had witnessed the most horrific and repugnant genocide it had ever known—six million Jews had been exterminated, and mankind was forever made aware that evil, unchecked, knows no limit.

Tension between Jewish immigrants and Muslim Arab Palestinians flared up with a vengeance. The Jews resorted to out and out TERRORISM as the most visible part of their strategy. During the period 1937 through 1948, three Jewish terrorist groups, Haganah, Irgun Zvai Leumi, and the Stern Gang were responsible for a series of bombings of Arabs, including women and children, and also of British authorities. These acts of terrorism occurred in market places, buses, private dwellings, hotels, etc. They even killed two hundred of their own when an attempt to prevent the deportation of three thousand Jews on SS *Patria* backfired. By this time, Britain had had enough, and, like Pontius Pilate two thousand years earlier, was eager to wash its hands off the whole mess.

Now America, who had always hovered about this stage, openly assumed the leading role. It is not unreasonable to assert that if Jewish wealth and power played such a big part during the First World War in getting Britain to open the door for Jews to emigrate, it just as certainly played a major role in ensuring American support of their goals, post-World War II. One must also assert that at no time during the period 1920–1948 had America made any effort to relax its strict immigration quotas, not even for the Jews fleeing Nazi Germany! America at that time had a large anti-Semitic faction too.

However, even the powerful Jewish lobby would not have succeeded then if America did not have a very powerful and receptive Christian faction which, as often happened in the course of history, was easily influenced by its extremist fundamentalists. Their belief in and interpretation of the Bible, coupled with having just witnessed the horror of the Holocaust, led them to support the Jews in Palestine. America, in the final days and months of talks and negotiations in the United Nations in 1947–1948, became the most ardent, indeed fanatical supporter of the notion that an independent Jewish state be created in Palestine as a home for the Jews.

Never mind that the reason the Jews were in such dire straits worldwide was that the Christians, not so much the Muslims, had, throughout the centuries, perpetrated atrocities against them and persecuted them, culminating in the Nazi holocaust. The Jews were eager to emigrate, and rightly so, considering the way they had been treated in all of Europe including Russia (Russia, too, had a long history of intolerance toward the Jews since the time they moved there, fleeing from European expulsions and pogroms over the ages)—a history that spilled over into the atheist Soviet era, despite the fact that many of the early Soviet Communist leaders and initiators were themselves Jews.

If you add to this the fact that public (Christian) opinion had been predisposed against the Muslims since time immemorial, you will see how the Palestinians never had a chance. Arguments have been made that not the whole population of Palestinians had ancestral roots in the land going back centuries, etc., but these are more in the way of distracting from the core fact that Palestine had been inhabited by a Muslim majority going back centuries. Why, the first Muslim to visit Palestine was Muhammad himself, and this was long after the Jews left back in 70 CE. It is said that he ascended into heaven from Jerusalem, at the site where the Dome of the Rock now stands.

America used every trick in the book, including some heavy-handed arm-twisting of some of the smaller members of the Unites Nations to finally wrest Resolution 181 from the General Assembly on November 29, 1947, partitioning Palestine into two states, one Jewish, and one Palestinian. The resolution called for British withdrawal by August 17, 1948, and the establishment of the two independent states by October 1, 1948. Arabs had rejected the plan on the grounds that it was unfair and violated their rights. For instance, it gave 56 percent of the land to the Jews who at that time owned only 7 percent and represented 33 percent of the population. Civil war immediately ensued, and Britain announced it would withdraw on May 15, 1948. Israel unilaterally declared statehood on May 15, and just *11 minutes later,* was recognized by the United States. Well, the conflict has gone on ever since—military, political, and terrorist conflict—with the Palestinians now being the ones resorting to terrorism against the Jews.

Fast forward sixty some years. Conflict still rages not only between Israel and Palestine, but the whole region is a powder keg. Though politics and economics have played a role in all of this, it is undeniable that a major role has been played by religion. To an atheist, it is one of the most tragic chapters in our history. A people who believe the land was given to them by their God comes back two thousand years after it was wrested from them to wrest it forcibly from another people who had lived there for centuries past, who, incidentally, got there because the prophet of their God (the same God of the first people, by the way) had conquered these lands. In fact, as stated earlier, this land is sacred to them too because it is from one of its cities, Jerusalem, that their prophet Muhammad ascended into heaven.

The extreme situations which religious beliefs are happy to support are terrifying. Israel now is reputed to have 250 nuclear bombs. Iran would dearly love to join the club. Iran's president, Ahmadinejad (2005–2013), stated publicly that he would like to see Israel wiped off the face of the earth. How's that for stirring the pot! Pakistan is already in the club (nuclear, that is). If Iran joins, Saudi Arabia will want to, and so on. Powder keg is clearly an understatement. Another holocaust waiting in the wings, perhaps? And sixty-plus years later, America's Christian majority are still as fervent as ever in their support, largely on religious grounds, of the need for Israel to exist. Some say that the real reason for the American support is that it needs another ally to protect its oil interests. Even if there was not a drop of oil in the Middle East, the American Jewish/Christian fundamentalist powerhouse would ensure that American support for Israel would continue indefinitely, and make a tough, lasting peace hard to come by.

This Palestinian problem has been the root cause of much that has gone wrong in the last sixty-plus years. Absent religion, the residual political-economic factors would be more amenable to solutions.

It could be argued that the very terrorism that besets Jews in the Middle East had been set up and exemplified in their own scriptures—indeed honored in one of their most sacred religious celebrations: Passover! I am sure that most people would be horrified that I say this, but please understand that I am merely presenting an interpretation of the situation so vividly described in the scriptures, without the blinkers of faith restricting me.

Passover celebrates the culmination of a terror campaign waged by GOD to secure the freedom of the Jews from Egypt. Just think about it. You have a God who, supposedly, is almighty. Clearly, if he so desired, he could have convinced the Egyptian pharaoh to free the Jews, or, if this suited him better, even forced him to. Instead he chose to wreak a campaign of terror on the whole Egyptian population, the likes of which have never been seen since. Let's take a look at it:

The Ten Plagues

The plague of blood. Contaminate the water supply, affecting the entire population. I would rate this as chemical warfare.

The plague of frogs. You can imagine the public pandemonium such an infestation would create. This could be considered biological warfare.

The plague of lice. Biological warfare too. Reported to have killed far more than one would imagine.

The plague of flies. Sometimes interpreted as wild animals(?). More biological warfare (or zoological?).

The plague of boils. Also interpreted as a skin rash. Germ warfare?

The plague of hail. Severe storms that hurt people and damaged crops and livestock. Meteorological warfare? Wow! Even today, we are incapable, I think, of waging this type of warfare. But who knows, maybe we are, but have just not used it, much less disclosed it!

The plague of locusts. Consumed all the remaining crops, leaving no tree standing. Biological warfare.

Plague of darkness. Total darkness for three days and nights. Demonstrates the Jewish God's power over Egypt's own Sun God, Ra. Not sure how to categorize this one. Technological warfare? Cosmic warfare, or perhaps space wars?

Death of firstborn. This the most terrifying of all the plagues—mass genocide, or holocaust?

These are forms of terrorism, pure and simple. Every one of these was directed, not against the rulers or power brokers or military leaders, but against the whole population. In every instance, the greatest number of victims was surely among the most vulnerable: the very old, the very young, and the very poor—totally indiscriminate. Particularly the last one which rained terror on absolutely every family without exception—something, I believe, that has never been done since, at least not on such a scale.

Of course I do not believe any of this actually happened, but, as I have said, Jews celebrate it, and so do the Christians believe in it. I have to admit that whenever such embarrassing, ridiculous tales are found in the scriptures, apologists hasten to explain that they are merely allegorical, or presented in a way that the audience of the time could relate to, and not to be taken literally, etc. I agree that scripture is not just the relating of fact and dogma, but the telling of stories in the form of parables, messages, and exhortations to encourage moral behavior. But parables and messages couched in these terms, describing these behavior choices by a being who, in his infinite power, could have chosen to act in a myriad other, more moral ways, do you not see human nature, not divine, at play here?

The message behind the Passover, forgetting whether it is literally true or not, is abundantly clear to an uninvolved observer. There are situations where violence IS justified to obtain political goals, and, in extreme situations, EVEN TERRORISM IS JUSTIFIED. I repeat, this is not my belief. I am merely pointing out that it's there, in our scriptures, for those who choose to believe them.

This has been acted out in human history time and time again. If your people is subjected to unimaginable injustice, you have a right to seek redress. If it becomes clear that there is absolutely no way justice will be meted out by peaceful, nonviolent means, then you are fully justified in escalating the confrontation to violence as a next step. Is this not what scripture would have us believe? In the Egypt of Moses it was clear. The Egyptians had one religion, and the Jews had another. The Egyptians were the masters, and the Jews servants. Moses was the only Jewish voice in court, albeit a powerful one. What chance was there of his pleas for his people's freedom falling on sympathetic or even impartial ears? They had no bargaining power at all—no army, no influence, nothing. In these circumstances, violence against official, more traditionally legitimate (military) targets was out of the question because the military could totally crush such attacks—for every Egyptian soldier killed a hundred Jews could perish (sound familiar?).

Guerrilla style warfare was probably also ruled out because you had the same problem: difficult to sustain and not likely to succeed against the all-powerful military. Indiscriminate terrorist activity would be considered as the only remaining option, one with its own set of perilous retributions, but with more probabilities of success, assuming the status quo of slavery as an option was never acceptable—which it was not. A campaign of terror followed and successfully resolved the situation.

Is this not similar to the world today? Take the Middle East situation. Again, not surprisingly, I keep coming back to the Middle East given the media attention it has received over the last sixty-eight years and given the real impact it has in world affairs. The Palestinians feel they were forcibly dispossessed of their land, and they are oppressed by an occupying force. They objected militarily and otherwise to the initial partition as being totally one-sided and disproportionate but were summarily neutralized. They complain of being treated as second-class citizens. Israel is one of the few remaining democracies with a state religion, Judaism, which is exclusive by definition. By the way, how many democracies do you know that have official state religions? All attempts to resolve the situation and achieve a sense of statehood by both negotiations and armed conflict have failed. The power of the Palestinians compared to Israel's is miniscule or nonexistent. The United Nations has proved ineffective. Their only meaningful court of appeals is the United States. Like the Egypt of biblical times, the United States also has a different religion with a long history of antagonism, to put it mildly, to that of the Palestinians, and their halls of power are filled with both Christians and Jews—not many sympathetic or impartial ears to hear the Palestinian cause. And if left to public opinion in the United States, the situation is just as bleak. Zero hope, then, of an acceptable peaceful outcome. Zero chance of the Jews giving up on what they consider to be theirs by divine right. Result? Terrorism.

Pity, considering that today, it is abundantly clear that a peaceful solution can be found if both parties are willing to compromise. And as I said earlier, before the Palestinian terrorists, we had the Jewish terrorists. Why, even Golda Meir and Menachem Begin were members of terrorist groups before Israeli independence, and Begin went on to win the Nobel Peace Prize—proof that terrorism presents itself as inevitable given the right (wrong?) circumstances.

But let us get back to morality. I guess what I am trying to show is that if religion is our only source for morality, it has done a lousy job at times. Religion has injected heightened confrontation into the Palestinian situation, and it has been abjectly incapable of imposing morality. If anything, the lack of morality from all sides is apparent—the powerful Jewish state shows a tendency to grab as much land as it can (justifying it as a necessary protective buffer, which, given its enmity with its neighbors, is understandable) and shows no compassion, and the weak Palestinians avail themselves of terror, using religion to motivate suicide bombers, and also show no willingness to compromise.

It would appear that the biblical passages on the scourges of Egypt read almost like a sanctioning of terrorism, and surely they do. The unfolding drama in the promised land seems to bear witness to that. For my part, I do not myself sanction terror nor does any reasonable person. But neither do I sanction the intransigence of the United States and Israel particularly when, in both cases, so much of it must ultimately be traced to their religious beliefs, religious superstitions, and religious ignorance.

Just think about it: If the United States were mostly Buddhist, would this situation have arisen? What I do see is the tragic irony in the situation. It is like truth emulating fiction—the truth of the Middle East emulating the fiction of the Bible. Of course, let it be clear that I do not sanction religious fanaticism from the Muslims either. Intransigence and fanaticism are suspect at all times, but when they spring from religion, they must be condemned with particular vehemence because religion, supposedly, is the source of morality. The only saving grace, if I could call it that, is that it appears that modern terrorists primarily act in the name of God. There is hope that once we are free of religion, we will see a significant drop in terror.

To those of you who rush to judgment and conclude that I am anti-Jewish or anti-Muslim, this is not the case at all. What I am is an atheist, and as such, do not recognize claims of the Jews to their "homeland" based on their religion, nor, for that matter to Jerusalem (Christians want this too, as it fits their biblical brain washing). I hear the cries of Jews saying Zionism has nothing to do with religion. Give me a break! If the Jewish people had not been indoctrinated for centuries in the "chosen people" and "promised land" myths (remember, I speak as an atheist), Zionists would have devised any one of a number of other solutions to the dire situations they were experiencing in Europe and Russia.

I am more inclined to recognize a right to a piece of land based on having lived there for the past several centuries than having once lived there close to two thousand years ago. I would also be prepared to entertain considerations of a homeland based on ethnicity and culture, but not religion per se. As I said earlier, if there is no GOD, no land has been promised. And there is no divine reason or right to occupy it, or any particular city in it, and then give it a state religion. Indeed, in this regard, I am really disappointed that Jewish atheists now and in the past have never spoken up on precisely this aspect of the Israeli problem, particularly given the fact that, percentage-wise, there is a substantial number of atheists among Jews, probably more than there are extremist, orthodox (should I say jihadist) Jews.

Einstein clearly stated that he did not believe in a personal God. It follows he clearly did not believe in the "promised land" or "chosen people"—both tenets of Jewish faith. *Yet even he never publicly said so,* as far as I know. He must have seen all the problems looming, yet kept silent. When he was offered the presidency of Israel after Ben Gurion's death, he naturally turned it down (wouldn't you, if you did not believe in the God of your nation's state religion?), but he could have used this as an excellent opportunity to speak up. Neither he nor any of the influential Jews before or since who are equally atheists or do not believe in a personal God have ever publicly stated the obvious. One would hope that privately they campaigned otherwise, but I have no knowledge of this. However, this is not surprising. How many influential Muslims have you heard speak out against terrorism? How many influential Christians spoke out against Hitler? How many atheists speak out and deny the concepts not only of the Jewish promised land but of the seventy virgins promised to jihadist martyrs? And most strange of all, what do the 15 percent or 16 percent of Israel's population who are atheist think of all this?

Nothing new here. The point I am making is that perhaps because more people do not speak up and express their true feelings, or because people do not bring true impartiality to the table, the terrorist alternative is the only one that presents itself to a desperate group with nowhere to turn to and in no mood to give up. And the point also is that RELIGION is very much at the core of the Middle East problem, and we are too blinded and influenced by it to be the ones handling the situation and holding the trump card (economic, and, ultimately, military force).

But again, I digress, at least to some extent. Let us get back to morality. *I would go so far as to state that morality itself is proof that God does not exist.* On close inspection, it quickly becomes obvious that morality, as espoused by religions throughout history, far from being the purest distilling of virtue by a perfect being presented to his imperfect creation, is nothing more than a reflection of the imperfections of the mere mortals it addressed. It becomes abundantly clear that morality in religion evolved as human society did—more or less in the right direction but with major and glaring gaps a God that holds virtues to be eternal could not have allowed.

For example, take slavery. Nowhere does the Bible explicitly condemn slavery, in fact it tacitly recognizes it almost as a given not only in the Old but also in the New Testament. I will not go into the arguments used to defend the Bible as they are quite inept and at times sadly pathetic. One fact stands out that is clear and is totally damning—slavery is not forbidden, period. You have the Ten Commandments that God etched in stone, his top ten list, if you please: do not kill, do not steal, do not commit adultery, and so on. There *is no* "do not take and hold slaves." How does scripture rate slavery compared to stealing, adultery, idolatry, bearing false witness, observing the Sabbath, or taking the Lord's name in vain? How do you, dear reader, rate slavery? Is it less evil than any of the above? Clearly, no, but scripture appears to suggest this.

I do not think anyone who considers himself a moral person would disagree with me that slavery is an absolute evil—no ifs, buts, or maybe. It is not something that is evil only in certain circumstances. It ranks way up there with all those other sins prohibited by religion, yet our religious texts nowhere demand we abstain from it. God feels it necessary to command men to observe the Sabbath but not to abstain from slavery? Did he think that man was not ready to appreciate the evil of slavery but could perceive the evil of, say, false testimony? What clearer proof is there that scriptures could not have been the work of God but of man, or the work of a God created by man? At the time they were written, man's morality had not progressed to the point of recognizing and accepting that the evil of slavery far outweighed any economic or other justification for it, so it was simply left out, tacitly recognizing and tolerating whatever perceived role it played in society. Man's morality evolved and will continue to evolve into the future. The God of the scriptures, however, if he was real, would have had then the same abhorrence of slavery that is now felt, and should have been as explicit about it then as he was of the other major sins. So I would argue that observing how morality appears in our scriptures clearly refutes any truly divine moral pedigree. If God saw fit to forbid stealing he could just as easily forbid the keeping of slaves. *The scriptures, like God, were created by man.*

Slavery still exists, sad but true. It is said there are more slaves today than at any time in our history. It is practiced in a much more insidious manner. There are sex slaves, debt slaves, and many other horrible forms prevalent in most societies—a continuing and telling indictment of God's and religion's failure to impose true morality. Let me just state here that while slavery is a blight on the human race, it is just one of many evils that man, not God, must eradicate from the face of the earth before he can realize the sublime virtue he ascribed to his Creator that is really the potential of his own species.

I have laid out clearly why I believe that God, *as we define him*, does not, or indeed, cannot exist, and that both God and religion are man-made. It is time to dwell on what this means. First, if man created God and religion and they are still pertinent today, it would be nice to believe that they have served us well. Remember, in creating God and religion, man poured his tremendous capacity for good and evil into his creations—God embodying all the good, and the devil all the evil. It is therefore appropriate, albeit somewhat stunning, to assume that religion and our belief in God has been used to explain, and in some cases promote, both good and evil—one in an obviously direct way, and the other indirectly and sometimes as a by-product, as in the waves of past persecutions and inquisitions. Most of the evil is attributed to the Devil or to man's straying from God, but unfortunately, a lot of the evil resulted from one faction's interpretation of its faith as being superior to the others, or at least so diametrically opposed to it that only force could redress the situation.

That is why at the beginning of this chapter, I said I would love to compile a balance sheet of religion: of how much good has it given us as opposed to bad. Unfortunately, I simply do not have the time or the stomach for this. Suffice it to say that I firmly believe that religion did in fact, at times, serve a quite useful purpose particularly in our early evolution, but, by its very nature, is proving tough to shed, long after it has become obsolete. As I said earlier, it is not easy to eradicate faith, especially when it is deeply ingrained in us from our very earliest memories as individuals and as a species. I am convinced, however, that change is afoot and will accelerate. According to the ARIS survey (American Religious Identification Survey) of 2008, 12 percent of Americans are either atheist or agnostic (more agnostic than atheist) and another 12 percent are deistic (do not believe in a personal God). This is close to double what it was eighteen years ago. It can be safely said that the world over, the majority of scientists reject the idea of a personal God. The rate of change, however, has slowed in the USA and Muslim countries and will continue to grow in Europe and the non-Muslim world.

Religion is obsolete because the personal God of religion makes for irrational policies at a local, insular level and dangerous confrontations and policies at the global level. Going forward, the complexity and interdependence of the global economy and society will increase even more dramatically. In the very close relations that will be necessary for good governance, REASON is the only imperative in the field. Reason must ultimately replace religion. Reason and the comfort that MORALITY is not God's doing but man's. Evil is not the Devil's work but ours. WE ARE IN CONTROL. Let us never forget that! This is why, as the title of this book suggests, THIS IS GOOD NEWS!

CHAPTER 4

SO WRONG FOR SO LONG?

> True wisdom comes to each of us when we realize how little we understand about life, ourselves, and the world around us.
>
> —Socrates

Inevitably, after reading the previous chapters, the realization hits us that when I say God does not exist and therefore all religions are mistaken, I am saying mankind has been mistaken ever since he walked the earth for it has been that long that he has believed in God and had religion. How could this be? Am I insane, or impossibly arrogant to suggest such a thing?

The answer, unfortunately, is a resounding no. First, not all men have believed at all times in God. Throughout the ages, atheists have existed, though they mostly remained under the radar for fear of reprisals from those who worshipped one God or another. Second, and more to the point, MANKIND HAS BEEN WRONG ABOUT MOST OF EVERYTHING MOST OF THE TIME. You name it! Our ideas about the world we live in, about our anatomy, about our origin, about disease, about just about anything and everything we observed were wrong until fairly recently in our history, and for good reason. Our intellectual powers, our knowledge base, the tools to develop the latter, and the ability to transfer it to future generations were simply not advanced enough to make the necessary breakthroughs. When breakthroughs finally were made, they were all too often met with severe opposition from entrenched interests, and this slowed progress even more. And so, it is not at all unusual that centuries, millennia, and indeed whole ages of man had passed before significant advances were made in dispelling fiction from fact.

Even where observational science was concerned, its discoveries were resisted with enormous pressure, especially where it was felt that, as a result, religious beliefs would be subjected to uncomfortable scrutiny. Just two examples illustrate this point.

In 1514 or earlier, Copernicus realized that the sun did not revolve around the earth but rather the other way around, yet it was not till the year of his death in 1543, some twenty-nine years later, that his finding was actually published. Not only did he wait till he was more confident of his theory and not only did he fear ridicule from his peers, but some scholars feel he feared religious repercussions—despite the very favorable receptions to his ideas from people like Pope Clement VII in 1533, and Cardinal Nikolaus von Schönberg in 1536.

His book is thought to have been fairly widely read, yet surprisingly, there was not much criticism of it at first. It was not until some six decades later, in that other giant, Galileo's, time, that the church woke up to its implications, and in 1616 "suspended" the book, pending correction, on the grounds that it went against scriptures to postulate that the earth moved and the sun was still, so to speak. In 1633, ninety years after Copernicus published, it was Galileo who was placed under house arrest for following in the footsteps of Copernicus! It is felt that the church's sudden reaction at this time was in part due to the fact that Galileo's assault was far more threatening because now it could actually be proven by telescopic observations! It was not until 1835 that the two books, Copernicus's *De Revolutionibus Orbium Coelestium* and Galileo's *Dialogue Concerning the Two Chief World Systems,* were removed from the Catholic

Church's list of prohibited books. *Revolutionibus Orbium Coelestium* was never actually suspended but merely withdrawn from circulation until phrases stating the earth's revolution as fact were modified to present them as merely hypotheses.

The point I am making is that since the dawn of time until quite recently (1543 is not that long ago in human history), all of us were wrong about the earth's position in the grand scheme of things—the universe! For thousands, not hundreds of years until quite recently, in fact, mankind had completely erroneous ideas about our physical world. Our sense of reality in these matters could not have been more distorted.

And it was not a big deal when, at last, we learned the truth! OK, I am sure that before this, there were times when some schools of thought contemplated a solar system closer to the truth, but these were short-lived exceptions. The most widely held and enduring belief was that the earth was still and the sun and stars revolved around it—the polar opposite of what we now know to be the truth. And we got over it! It did not shatter our way of life, and we survived quite well, thank you. We even prospered, despite what the church would have us fear! Another misbelief related to this was that the earth was flat. This misbelief, however, was not held as long as the earth-centric belief. It is well-documented that the ancient Greeks postulated a spherical earth, but many other ancient cultures did believe the earth was flat for much longer.

The second example is Darwin's work on EVOLUTION. In this case, there was no immediate and serious reaction from the religious establishment. The days and fears of the Inquisition were long gone, though the Roman inquisition officially ended in 1860, a year after Darwin published his book *On the Origin of Species.* But yet even today, evolutionary theory is hotly contested by religious believers in CREATIONISM. In the United States, a bastion of orthodox religious beliefs, there have been efforts at state and local levels to blunt the teaching of evolutionary science in schools. In this regard, there is an uncanny resemblance to the "corrections" that were required in

Copernicus and Galileo's published works. Disclaimers were required stating that evolution is just a theory, not scientific fact!

Here is a sticker that appeared in biology textbooks in Cobb County, Georgia, USA:

> This textbook contains material on evolution. Evolution is a theory, not a fact, regarding the origin of living things. This material should be approached with an open mind, studied carefully, and critically considered.
>
> Approved by
> Cobb County Board of Education
> Thursday, March 28, 2002

A federal judge later ordered the stickers removed.

Alabama, Arkansas, Florida, Georgia, Kansas, Kentucky, Louisiana, Michigan, New Mexico, Ohio, Pennsylvania, South Carolina, Texas and Wisconsin—fourteen states in all, have either had restrictions (some still do) of one kind or another placed on the teaching of evolution in schools, or controversial decisions relating to the teaching of alternate theories (creationism), or refer to evolution as theory, not fact. This has not all been statewide as some of it was at a very local level.

Note that most of these states are Southern, and remember that in the last few elections in the United States, some of the so-called battleground states casting the deciding votes (Florida and Ohio) were in the above "creationist" group. If this is what brings our presidents to power, what kind of agendas can we expect from them? Severely curtailing stem cell research, linking federal aid to anti-abortion policies, and providing funds to control AIDS in Africa and other countries with religious-inspired strings attached. To quote from the Eugene, Oregon, *Register-Guard,* June 3, 2006:

The heavy handed intrusion of religious ideology into AIDS prevention efforts is affecting how money is spent without regard to local needs. The problem is the Bush Administration's insistence, written into law by a terrible Republican spending amendment, that one third of all funds be used to emphasize sexual abstinence and fidelity.

The same article later states: "Gone, at the Bush administration's insistence, from a new draft of a United Nations action plan is any mention of the word 'condom' and all references to providing clean syringes to drug users." On top of this, there was a global gag rule which prevented funds from going to any organization that either offered or counseled on abortion. What puritanical arrogance! In an ideal world, every congressman linked to such an outrageous amendment hopefully would be pilloried at the polls. What the elections did bring, thankfully, was an administration that promised "best practice, not ideology" and gagged the gag rule, and by all accounts, the Bush Aid Program in Africa has been a huge success.

Forgive my digression, but it is so infuriating and so easy to get sidetracked. However, I hope you are beginning to see how mankind has, in the past, held on to a belief for centuries only to drastically alter it when new evidence presented itself: when knowledge gradually accreted over time, sometimes suddenly in discrete leaps, to reveal a new reality in sharp, unmistakable relief.

As I said in the beginning, our whole interpretation of the physical world had to be flawed almost by definition. As Stephen Hawking likes to say, "Nothing in this universe is perfect," and man certainly is not. As I said earlier, too, you name it, and we were wrong about it. Anything! Take lightning and thunder. Do you recall the fantastic interpretations our distant forebears gave to these phenomena? Lightning was viewed as an attribute of a god or as a god itself. Zeus used the thunderbolt as a weapon. In Judaism, a blessing should be recited when lightning is seen. And so on. It was not till the eighteenth century that Ben Franklin's experiments began to shed light on the phenomenon, and it was not till the beginning of the last century that our understanding of lightning really developed due to the need to protect power transmission lines and equipment. How many eons did it take us in this case to discover the truth behind lightning?

The point to remember is that where the physical world is concerned, it is relatively easy to accept new ideas when they are presented because they can be rigorously tested and confirmed using well-established scientific method. Take the big bang for instance. Theories about the origins of the universe have been legion in our history. Not surprising. This and the origin of life are by far the most enthralling subjects out there (the *purpose* of life is in another league all by itself). In the case of the big bang, I won't go into a detailed history of it here, having briefly described it in chapter 1, but here is a summary of events leading to its acceptance.

In 1927, George Lemaître published a report that showed a radially expanding universe and derived what became known as the Hubble law (this law basically states that the velocity with which a galaxy is traveling away from ours is proportional to its distance from us, or v=Hd, where H is the Hubble constant which varies with time). At a meeting in 1931 of the British Association, he proposed that the universe expanded from an initial point at an initial moment in time. Fred Hoyle later sarcastically dubbed this the big bang.

In cosmology, our hypotheses are stated and developed as mathematical formulas and equations. From these, further mathematical derivations are made, and outcomes or predictions are determined. Only when these outcomes are subsequently confirmed by physical observations is the hypothesis accepted by the scientific community. Among the predictions associated with the big bang theory are the existence of the cosmic microwave background, an abundance of primordial elements, galactic evolution and distribution, a homogeneous and isotropic universe, and so on. Enough of these have in fact been verified to make this the most currently held theory of the origin of the universe.

So the answer to the question posed at the beginning of this chapter is yes, we could have been wrong for so long because we have been wrong about most of everything else. So why, you ask, do you think you are right this time? Because we are at a point in time when our knowledge has advanced to a stage where we are sufficiently confident about the conclusions drawn from science and scientific method and observation. And MORE IMPORTANTLY, WE KNOW, just as confidently, WHAT MUST BE WRONG. We did not have this confidence before because we did not have this track record of discovery and advancement in knowledge. Proof of our achievements is all around us. From landing on the moon to splitting the atom, from curing diseases to creating life in a test tube, there is irrefutable evidence that we have advanced to a higher state of knowledge and awareness than ever before. So yes, based on what we now know of the origins of the universe, the origin of our species, our morality, and so on, we are confident in our realization that our ideas about God and religion were wrong—well intentioned, maybe, but wrong!

But it is a good question nonetheless. There is a school of thought that believes that man is reaching the limits of his intellectual ability. That it could conceivably result that the remaining amount of knowledge of the universe out there is so vast and complex as to be beyond the physical capacity of the human brain to assimilate and comprehend. If this is true, then it is possible that we may never know with absolute certainty what the truth is, but could reasonably assess what it is not.

In other words, if you fear that having been wrong for so long in the past we could just as easily be wrong now, the answer is yes, CERTAINLY, WE CAN STILL BE WRONG, but because of the exhaustive scrutiny and rigid evaluation given to modern scientific theories, there is every chance that any weaknesses in scientific hypotheses are soon discovered, published, and discussed in the public forum. PERHAPS THE BEST SAFEGUARD WE HAVE AGAINST REPEATING MISTAKES OF THE PAST IS IN PRESERVING A FREE AND OPEN SOCIETY. EVEN SCIENTISTS SHOULD BE KEPT HONEST.

CHAPTER 5

A BRIEF OVERVIEW OF MAJOR RELIGIONS

> I believe in the fundamental Truth of all great religions of the world. And I believe that if only we could, all of us, read the scriptures of the different Faiths from the stand-point of the followers of those faiths, we should find that they were at the bottom, all one and were all helpful to one another
>
> —Mahatma Gandhi

I apologize in advance if this chapter or any part of this book is particularly offensive to some. It is not my intention to disrespect others. I believe that all people are deserving of respect, and that people are entitled to their belief systems. I myself am by no means an expert or scholar in this field (religions) but I hope you will understand that, from my point of view as an atheist, I tend to view religions like any other phenomena of human society, to be evaluated in a completely dispassionate manner. I will try to present them in nothing but a cold, analytical, dispassionate, and detached light. I believe that freedom of expression is vital to the advance of civilization, but it must be exercised with responsibility and respect for the opinion of others.

At the outset, let me repeat that I myself was born a Christian. A Catholic to be precise. When did I change? I guess I started questioning this whole area when I was in my teens. But I would drift in and out of faith without firmly committing to one side or the other. It wasn't till I was in my fifties that I considered myself officially in the third ranked category of the list of religions below: "secular, agnostic, atheist, non-religious." In my sixties, I realized that within that category, I was more atheist than anything else. I am now in my seventies, and still a staunch atheist. It is entirely possible that, human nature being what it is, in my final years I shall revert to a belief in the afterlife, particularly as my end nears and the prospect of just turning into dust is unappealing. Such is the nature of man!

But enough about me and back to the subject of this chapter. What follows is a list of the major religions in the world today ranked by size (number of followers) from the adherents.com website. Unfortunately, the site does not date it (don't you just hate that?). Why, for God's sake (forgive the usage, force of habit), do people not date their postings? Ten or twenty years from now, how on earth can we assess the date of statistics such as these, and hence their relevance? Anyway, I accessed the site in May 2010, and they were referred to then as "current estimates" with some of its sources dated 2001. Also, they relate pretty closely to other estimates such as the *Wikipedia's* major religious groups page, Pew studies, etc. that were consulted around May 2010 too. Finally, I like them because they include the category "secular."

In the original list, Juche was ranked tenth with 19 million people, practically the whole population of North Korea. Juche refers to the ideological "regime" imposed on the North Korean people as a result of the Sino-Soviet split of the 1960s to preserve their ideological communist orthodoxy. For the purposes of this discussion, I consider Juche as part of the secular category, as its basic tenet is man controls his own destiny without any interference whatsoever from supernatural entities. Here is the list:

Religion	Followers
1. Christianity	2.1 billion
2. Islam	1.5 billion
3. Secular (agnostic, atheist, non-religious)	1.1 billion
4. Hinduism	900 million
5. Chinese traditional	394 million
6. Buddhism	376 million
7. Primal – indigenous	300 million
8. African traditional and Diasporic	100 million
9. Sikhism	23 million
10. Spiritism	15 million
11. Judaism	14 million
12. Baha'i	7 million
13. Jainism	4.2 million
14. Shinto	4 million
15. Cao Dai	4 million
16. Zoroastrianism	2.6 million
17. Tenrikyo	2 million
18. Neo-paganism	1 million
19. Unitarian Universalism	800 thousand
20. Rastafarianism	600 thousand
21. Scientology	500 thousand

You may be surprised by the number of people classified as secular. Don't be! Is it not more likely that from the very beginning of the evolution of religion there have been skeptics? Since religion basically evolved as an explanation or way to cope with the enormous gaps in our understanding of the universe and our role in it, it is clear that from the very beginning, there were differing views—skeptics of every hue and color. I believe that, hopefully, what is happening is that this ever present base of skeptics is now growing more vigorously, aided first by the increased freedom prevailing in societies, second, by the increasing failure of religion in the modern world, and, lastly, by vastly increasing knowledge and understanding available to us that so successfully and efficiently dispels the fog religion often drapes over the world. So what are these religions about? Let me try to give you a summary of each of the major religions—a very rudimentary, and I hope, respectful understanding of each. It is the least I can do, considering—

Christianity

Let us start with, what else, Christianity, the largest bloc, by far, and the most widespread. Christians believe that Jesus of Nazareth is God made man for the salvation of mankind. There is only one God, the same God of the Jews and Muslims, but he exists and manifests as a Trinity: the Father, the traditional and primary image of God and the Creator of the universe and Father of all beings; the Son, the aforementioned Jesus of Nazareth who took our form and died for us to prove his love for us, to atone for our sins, and thereby provide for our salvation; and the Holy Spirit, who proceeds from the Father and the Son but is one with them, and performs such spiritual works in man as "conviction of sin," repentance, conversion, and the "grace" to live a righteous life. I know this is a very rushed and ridiculously brief summation, but a more in-depth exposition is beyond the scope of this book. As I suggested elsewhere, I urge you to consult other sources for a more complete understanding of the various religions.

The coming of the Son, also known as the Messiah, was prophesied in the Old Testament. The Christian Old Testament is based on Greek, Latin, or other translations of the Hebrew Tanakh, starting a few centuries BC in the case of the Greek translations. Besides the Old Testament, Christians have the New testament, a collection of works written at different times after the crucifixion of Jesus by different authors, comprising twenty-seven volumes of which the most important are the four gospels (of the apostles of Jesus: Matthew, Mark, Luke, and John) and the letters of Paul of Tarsus. As a kid growing up, I was unaware that there were twenty-seven volumes, and still cannot name all of them. My recollection is limited to the four gospels, the letters to the disciples, and maybe a few more.

Over the years, all religions, including Christianity, have changed and evolved both within themselves and with regard to the religions from which they sprang. While Christianity sprang from Judaism, it is claimed by Jews that mistranslations and misinterpretations occurred of the original versions of the Jewish texts (for example, in some passages, *young woman* in the Jewish text is translated as "virgin" in the Christian version of the Old Testament, and this is said to be the source of the "virginity" attributed to Mary, the mother of Jesus). However, it would still be fair to say that despite translation discrepancies and so on, Christianity really does share the Jewish scripture, thus many of their basic beliefs are shared.

Where they part ways is in the belief regarding the Messiah. Simply put, Jews do not believe the Messiah has come while Christians do, and of course, the whole body of theology related to the Christian Messiah is anathema to the Jews. But both believe in one God, the Ten Commandments, an eternal soul, an afterlife where a good life is rewarded (heaven), and that a bad life must be atoned for (purgatory in Christianity and gehinnom in Judaism), and so on. One major difference is the concept of hell. Jews, I am told, do not believe in eternal punishment (hell) but Christians do. One school of thought in Christianity believes hell is more a place of eternal separation from God than eternal physical torture and fire. It is, nonetheless, a very murky aspect of Christianity and difficult to reconcile with the rest of the Christian script. Suffice it to say that only the truly unrepentant, in a state of mortal sin, will go to hell. The definition of mortal sin is by no means absolute either—there is no list of them as far as I know. They are, however, grievous transgressions from the moral code committed with full knowledge and consent. Obvious ones are those in the Ten Commandments: idolatry, blasphemy, adultery, murder, and less obvious ones are theft (what is stolen and from whom?), extramarital sex, and so on. Another very thorny aspect of Christianity is that eternal salvation can be obtained only through Christ. Christian theologians agonize over explaining this away, saying, essentially, that Christ, by dying on the cross, did indeed make salvation available to all mankind—so even non-Christians who live a virtuous life will, in fact, be saved thanks to Christ's sacrifice. (Is this akin to Jews explaining away the idea of "chosenness" as meaning "called to testify and witness" so as not to sound offensive and superior to others?)

While this makes perfect sense per se, it smacks of serious backpedaling to explain away the apparent exclusiveness of salvation through Christ claimed in all the many grim pronouncements on the subject dating back to earliest Christian times. The fact is, in most religions, the vast majority of believers have very distorted and erroneous views of their own theology and even more distorted views of religions other than their own. Most religions, if not all, have passages in their scriptures that contradict their stated beliefs. And most theologians hasten to proffer the most ingenious workarounds when this surfaces, including misinterpretation or translation error.

Christians, naturally, in my view at least, pay more attention to the New Testament, based, as it is, on the life and teachings of Jesus, the Messiah. If I were asked to identify a major difference between the Old and New Testaments, I would say this: the New Testament's theme is softer, and the Old Testament's theme is harsher despite some exceptions, one of which was mentioned above—the concept of hell. Also, the Old Testament is concerned more, but not exclusively, with one particular "chosen" group of people, and the New Testament embraces the whole world. When I say "softer," there is much more talk of forgiveness, turning the other cheek, compassion for the less fortunate, etc. in the New Testament, at least in the four gospels, and less talk of an eye for an eye (yes, I know that this expression is also used to ensure that the retribution is not greater than the crime, at least this is what is claimed, or is this another case of backpedaling?), fire and brimstone (some extreme Christian sects, of course, do preach fire and brimstone), catastrophic punishments visited on sinners, on whole cities and nations, etc. This is stunningly illustrated in the Sistine Chapel in the Vatican. On one side, you see harsher scenes from the Old Testament, and on the other, more benign scenes from the New Testament—the flow from the Old Covenant and Mosaic law to the New Covenant and the Christian doctrine.

In Christianity, as in most every religion, afterlife beliefs provide the incentive for leading a virtuous life. It has even been argued that this incentive to live a virtuous life clearly contributes to group survival. This useful, secular by-product, advancing group survivability, became and has been one of the main drivers for the continuing survival and evolution of religion!

The above also supports the hypothesis that scriptures reflect the mores of the times they were written in: first, the later the date of their authorship and the more advanced the civilization at the time, the more refined and emancipated they become (reflecting the progress made by the contemporary civilization), and, second, this trend would be expected if men were in fact the authors and not God (they would relate to what could be known and imagined at the time of writing). If God were the author, why don't we see revelations that contemporary authors could not possibly have imagined and only future generations could have conceived?

All of this aside, if it were not for the fact that Emperor Constantine of Rome embraced the Christian faith and legalized it in AD 313, it is not at all clear that Christianity would be the widely practiced religion it is today. (Some, like Edward Gibbon, have even suggested that Christianity played a role in the *fall* of the Roman empire, but I tend to side with those that do not see enough evidence for this.)

Unfortunately, one of the issues I have with religion surfaced just seventy-eight years after this milestone event when, in AD 391, Rome made the worship of other Gods illegal! Here you have a group which believed in tolerance, compassion, and all those "softer" virtues of the New Testament, a group that was persecuted horribly for years and therefore knew what intolerance was, turn around and forbid other forms of worship! But of course, their Old Testament demanded, in the first of the Ten Commandments, no less, that "You shall have no other gods before me." Does this also explain why the Jews, who had suffered persecutions like never before in history, turned around and created a state with their religion as the "official" religion (i.e. their God as the only God), and who are seen by some to discriminate against other faiths in that state and by others, to practice a kind of apartheid as it were? All because it is one of their commandments? No, I do not believe this to be the case, but I would be remiss if I fail to see the role played by religion; and I believe the orthodox Jews, who are fortunately in a minority, hold extreme views that could indirectly permeate and influence Israeli society and politics.

From a commonsense perspective, it is not so surprising to this observer that Christianity won the day in Rome and many other days since. Because of the great message of comfort and joy it brings, backed up by simple but effective afterlife incentives, it is not surprising that it attracted the masses. It is also the opinion of this observer that Christianity has not lived up to its promise. Its spiritual leaders became so caught up in the lure of temporal power and the need to protect their status that they abused their authority and their followers. A religion based on salvation and love for all people turned in on itself and became mired in persecutions as vile as those of the Romans hundreds of years earlier. The medieval Inquisitions first, which raged on and off from 1184 through the 1230s, and the Spanish Inquisition later, starting in 1478 and not officially ending till 1834, have to rank among the darkest annals of the church, and I dare say, humanity!

This period is a clear example of how any type of censorship, particularly if imposed by religion, stifles human progress and literally creates a hell on earth. This is why I ask that even if you disagree with my views, you respect my right to state them! Do not constrain full and open discourse. I am trying to be as analytical and impartial as I can.

Anyway, I repeat, Christianity has not been all bad. At some point, some of those beautiful concepts embraced by the religion had to work their magic and they did. The church did not just spread the faith, but it also brought education, cared for the sick and needy, social welfare work, and other beneficent works wherever it went. Many saintly people, inspired by their beliefs, accomplished tremendous humane achievements. A fairly recent example is Mother

Theresa of India. I will not go into details of the tremendous sacrifices made by people such as these and the tremendous work they did. That could be the subject of many other books.

Even the Jesuits, maligned as they have been in some sectors, have been a tremendous force for good. In South America, they kept the natives from becoming slaves, and, possibly, from being decimated. They introduced Western science into China and educated Europe in Chinese culture, literature, and philosophy. They established centers of learning and universities in countries throughout the world that are highly regarded till this day.

Over the centuries, the work of Christian missionaries in caring for the sick, needy, and outcasts must also be recognized. Just one example: the work of Father Damien, a Belgian priest who tended to the lepers in the island of Molokai from 1873 till he died in 1889, having contracted the disease himself. Why, I can remember that even I, as a kid, went through a stage where I felt inspired by him and would have pursued a like calling myself but was not enough of a believer to follow through. Anyway, reason had started to peck away at my religious faith. Does this mean reason cannot do the good works that faith can? Not at all! Reason can, in fact, do a better job. Nations and NGOs can help other nations' sick and needy with no religious strings attached. Oxfam is a secular organization and among its founders one can find both religious figures and humanists. The Red Cross is similarly a humanitarian organization first and foremost—religious persons are welcome, of course. The point is that, yes, faith can accomplish wonders, but this does not mean secularism will fall short, by any means.

I readily admit that faith can indeed move mountains. It would be foolhardy to deny this. It would be tantamount to asserting that certain drugs do not induce behavioral changes. An apt comparison, I think, because faith does indeed act like a drug. I accept the power and potential of faith wholeheartedly, as proof, not of divine intervention, but of man's own capability to soar to the same thresholds of behavior that he himself established for the deity he conceived. Religion provides the crutch that we use to walk the walk. Learning to walk on our own will not be easy. Let us not kid ourselves. Using the drug allegory again, losing religion will be like rehabilitation from drugs with all the dangers of withdrawal that come with this. But do it we must if we are to walk out of the shadows cast by religion into the light of man's own reason. And there are signs that we are learning to do this.

Finally, to get back to Christianity, there is the legacy of magnificent architecture, art, and music bequeathed by this and most other faiths. I hope it is clear I am not acting as an apologist for any of the religions I deal with here. If anything, the opposite is true, so at some point in my brief description of each, I will raise the question: If this religion is so good and virtuous, how come...? In the case of Christianity, the "how come" question is on slavery. How come Christianity tolerated slavery from the beginning? It does not count that toleration of slavery was inherited from Judaism and Roman society. If slavery is wrong today, it was wrong a hundred or a thousand or two thousand years ago, yet our religion did not share that conviction till fairly recently. As a religion, we erred in the past. If we erred *then*, can we be erring *now*? I can go on and on about both the good and the bad that Christianity has given us, but that is not the purpose of this book. Let me just try and get to some of the other religions on the list.

Islam

While Christianity clearly is a natural extension or a branching out of Judaism, starting with the fulfillment of the Messianic prophecy, Islam's claim is that it represents the definitive completion of the faith revealed in the past, particularly to the prophets Abraham and Moses, and, later, to the "prophet" Jesus. Feeding this belief is the realization that in Islam the Koran represents the direct word of God spoken specifically and intimately in Arabic. While the Jewish and Christian scriptures are mostly in a historical, narrative, descriptive, and mostly third person format, the Koran is mostly God speaking in the first person directly to his prophet, and, through him, directly to his people. In its native language, it is said to be beyond compare, simply awesome, and there is nothing close! But translated into other languages, the Koran is, if anything, less compelling than Christian and Jewish scriptures. For this reason, Muslims the world over prefer to stick with Arabic to read and recite the Koran, rather than translate it into their individual languages and lose so much in the translation. In Arabic, it is quite simply the voice of God exactly as Muhammad heard it. The Koran is the voice of God himself communicating his message directly with no room for error, thus completing and tying up any loose ends the Jewish and Christian scriptures may have left.

Islam believes in the God of the Jews (but rejects the Trinity of the Christians), in angels, and messengers of God (the prophets, of which Muhammad is the one to whom God's final message, including the verses of the Koran, was revealed, speaking through the angel Gabriel). Muslims also believe in the day of judgment and the eternal soul (even animals have them). Heaven is restricted to Muslims only, and hell is unequivocally for nonbelievers. Heaven and hell are graphically described in Muslim scriptures. I wish it were otherwise, but as I said earlier, I am not an expert in this or any other religion and merely present what I find by researching the subject as impartially and dispassionately as I can, although I can truly say that I have had, and still have, close Christian, Jewish, Muslim, and Hindu friends.

If the concept of heaven and hell are powerful incentives in the Christian faith, they are even more so in Islam. Muslims see heaven and hell as real places, graphically described with every glorious or ghoulish detail. Islam is also the most exclusive of religions (more so than Judaism) in that it is pretty clear that nonbelievers are condemned to hell. The other side of the coin is that Allah forgives believers all their sins with the exception of two, *kufr* (disbelief) and *shirk* (ascribing divinity to others). Thus all Muslims can avail themselves of this mercy and get to heaven. This must apply also to those Muslims who misguidedly kill people, innocent or not, in their various jihads and fatwas. At least that's how jihadists must interpret it.

Though Muslims do not explicitly believe in the Ten Commandments, there are verses in the Koran that, taken individually, parallel each of the Ten Commandments. So, basically, I would say that while Islamic morality is very similar to the other major so-called monotheistic religions, it is much more categorical at all levels about only believers going to heaven, whereas nonbelievers, even though they may be rewarded in this life for good deeds, will nonetheless be condemned to hell in the hereafter. In this sense, it is a much more rigid and inflexible affair. Anyway, why bother rewarding the good nonbelievers in this life only to condemn them to eternal damnation in the afterlife?

It would also appear that Islam today is far more sensitive to serious infringements of code than we are in the West. I would even suggest that it is more sensitive now than it was in the past. It is here that the "justice" principle of an eye for an eye can be appreciated. In Islam, the punishment meted out often far exceeds the crime compared to other religious cultures, at least today. It's more like two eyes for one!

Given the timing of this book, and following on the latter observation, it is imperative to dwell on the role played by Islam on the world stage in terms of terrorism. Terrorism has always been around. As I said in an earlier chapter, the freeing of the Jews from Egypt, if it ever happened, was a campaign of terror waged by God Himself. There is no archaeological evidence that the exodus ever occurred despite television documentaries to the contrary, whereas there exists archaeological material from contemporaneous Egyptian and other cultures/religions in the same geographic area. In modern times, the Jews practiced terror tactics against the British and Arabs in Palestine (OK, mostly against the British military), and the Palestinians have been using terrorism ever since. The recent trend in jihad, however, that launched on 9/11/2001, has established a new paradigm in terrorism.

It is natural and welcome to see Islamic scholars hasten to point out that Islam is a peaceful religion and that a few extremists have hijacked their religion to buttress and use their terrorism for mostly secular purposes. I am inclined to agree with them. But truth be told, Islam has always been both a peaceful religion and a violent one. Witness the substantial use of force in its initial propagation and throughout its history, when doing so was readily justified as acting in God's name or in defense of faith. Violence for any other reason is prohibited. Heaven knows that we currently have, and have had, our fair share of extremists in the Christian faith. Look around and you will uncover them in the Hindu, Jewish, Buddhist, and other faiths too. However, given the ingrained practice in Sharia law of severe and radical punishment far exceeding the crime, one must accept both a predisposition and a resignation in Islamic society to the violence seen in jihad (a case in point is the practice of public beheadings in some Muslim societies mirrored by terrorist beheadings before video cameras). Could this be the reason that even though there has been strong and resounding criticism of violent jihad from within the Islamic community in many Western nations, though nowhere near enough, it has been somewhat lacking in those countries that are home to, if not havens for the terrorist groups? Polls increasingly show that support for Islamic extremism is waning in major Muslim populations, and more and more Imams are speaking out against it, some even issuing fatwas against Islamic terrorism. Dr. Tahir-ul-Qadri from Pakistan issued a six hundred-page fatwa attacking Al-Qaeda's ideology in every detail and in no uncertain terms. He even rejected views that self-martyrdom is justified in certain situations as in the injustice suffered by the Palestinians at the hands of Israelis. This was in March 2010, and there have been others before and since. Hopefully it will be, and it must be, from within that Islamic extremism will be finally silenced.

The sad truth is that Islam today is a far cry from its golden age from the mid-eighth to the mid-thirteenth, perhaps fifteenth century—lasting some five hundred to seven hundred years. During this time, the Islamic empire, led initially by Muhammad himself, rapidly acquired and ruled over territory extending all the way from Spain in the west to across the North African continent on through all of the Middle East, including what is today Saudi Arabia, into

Turkey, Afghanistan, Pakistan, and India, into parts of what are the Central Asian Islamic states today, and parts of Southeastern Europe. Perhaps, as it is sometimes stated, some of the gloss attributed to Islam during this era is overkill and the result of apologists going overboard in defending Islam. However, there is little doubt that in the Islamic empire, Christian, Jewish, and other cultures continued to prosper under Muslim rule; and mathematicians, philosophers, scribes, and businessmen of all cultures, including Islam, bequeathed and transferred to the West major troves of knowledge which became giant stepping stones for advances in philosophy, science, medicine, economy, agriculture, industry, and technology. While medieval Europe was self-destructing and losing its way, the Muslim world was quietly and steadily amassing knowledge that would be passed on to the West and allow for a transition to the Renaissance.

From its very inception, when Muhammad lived in Medina, the Jews and Christians were treated as their equals and had complete freedom to practice their faith. The much maligned harsh laws—stoning to death for adulterers and chopping off an arm for thieves—were more intended to drive home the seriousness of the crime than actually inflict the punishment. The death sentence for adultery required at least four unimpeachable direct witnesses, and in the case of robbery, a more lenient punishment was meted out if committed due to need. In those early centuries, women were treated as equals and were only required to dress *modestly*—nowhere near the modern extremes found in the Arab world. Islam is democratic at its core, recognizing equality among sexes, classes, and races. Islam, through the Koran and the Hadith (teachings drawn from Muhammad's words and actions), lays out a detailed guide on how to lead your daily life both as an individual and a society. Nothing is left to doubt. It worked and produced an open, progressive society and an empire unlike any other before or since. It is indeed a tragedy that today Islam is but a shadow of its glorious past. Unfortunately, like the other major religions, it too has failed to change for the better as human society evolved. In fact Islam has found it more difficult to change because of its fundamental premise—that of being based on God's directly spoken words.

But as the saying goes, nothing is certain except change, and change has indeed occurred, mostly for the worse. Islam has reacted to the forces of change by retrenching inward and becoming totalitarian where democracy previously held sway, inquisitional and persecutory where freedom of worship was the norm, harsh with punishment and stingy with forgiveness, a denier of human rights to women where full equality of women was possible, tolerant of corruption, cheating and lying where transparency, truth, and honesty were in evidence, and prone to exclusiveness instead of an all-inclusive society. Alas, it would seem that the divide between Islam and the world is becoming greater with each passing decade, adding fuel to the "clash of civilizations" alarmists.

Enter the recent phenomenon of the Arab Spring, which should give us pause and hope that change for the better is at hand in the Muslim world! The same democracy, human rights, equality, transparency, and participation alluded to earlier are major factors behind the movement for change we have been witnessing. Is it naive to hope that these are signs that Islam is on the verge of a renaissance and a return to its glorious days of yore? Alas, I fear that to be the case. In times like these, however, it is even more important to *not* be swayed by hate talk and paint all Muslims with the same brush used by an extremist, Muslim-hating minority. We should not even judge Islam based on the words and actions of out-of-touch rulers and out-of-step ayatollahs who have painted themselves into a dark and murky corner. We should learn for ourselves and remember what Islam is really about, working with the vast, peaceful Muslim majority. Before giving up on Islam, let us remember that there are some Islamic states that appear to be transitioning quite favorably into the modern era. Turkey is one example, though struggling with it, I admit. Indonesia is another, perhaps Morocco and Tunisia too?

For a more thorough understanding of the beauty of Islam, I would recommend Huston Smith's *The World's Religions*. While he eloquently describes Islam as it was and should be, I should also point out that Islam currently has some very vocal dissidents from within. Irshad Manji is one of them, a Canadian citizen who is outspoken in her criticism of the direction her faith has taken and is being taken.

This is a good time to point out that the failures of religion we see throughout history have resulted, practically every time, from religious institutions screwing up and woefully mishandling and abusing their power and stature. Rarely have they resulted from the values themselves associated with the religions. The difference between principle and practice is like night and day. This is the major reason for agnosticism. People are turned away from the institution of the church. In Catholicism, for instance, where on earth did the idea of selling indulgences come from all those centuries ago? Even if it "made sense" when correctly applied (a genuinely good deed will serve as penance and reduce your temporal punishment in the after-life for venial sins), where did the church get the authority to trade good deeds or whatever for time spent in "purgatory"? Why were good deeds equated to cash donations? Where did the concept of purgatory and venial sins come from anyway! Follow these with the abuses in *selling* indulgences, and you have the Protestant revolution! A classic example of institutions running wildly out of control.

Before I leave Islam, here is my how come question: The hijacking of Islam by a few fanatics, ayatollahs or otherwise, is a far greater assault on it than any perceived or real threat from others. How come Islam remains powerless to address this? Will the Arab Spring begin to turn the tide? Where is the outrage from within?

Hinduism

I will not tire of repeating here, again, that I am not a scholar of religion, much less the more exotic (in the Western view) religions. However, let me state my impressions from what I have read and heard and from my close exposure over the years to Hindus and their culture. Unlike the other monotheistic religions, Hinduism is more a way of life than a religion, although this is also true of Judaism for many, not all, Jews. In fact, the Sanskrit term for Hinduism, *sanatana dharma*, means *eternal law* or *eternal way*. It is certainly among the oldest religions, perhaps the oldest extant religion, considering that it was a natural product or derivation of ancient Brahmanic and Vedic traditions dating back to India's Iron Age around 1100 to 350 BC. There is no single founder, no central authority, nor are the sacred texts viewed in the same light of literal absolutism common in the other major religions. I am not aware of a list of commandments similar to the Ten Commandments of the Judeo-Christian tradition. The moral precepts are scattered through thousands of verses of text and narrative. Hindu sacred texts are viewed more as guides written in metaphor than verbatim revelations or personal and direct injunctions of the supreme being. Many Hindus, in fact, view these texts as an exposition by mere mortals of the spiritual laws they were capable of appreciating and developing without the need for divine intervention. In this sense, Hinduism comes close to what atheists have always stated—that morality has been conceived by and created for mankind.

This may explain why heresy is not an issue in Hinduism: there is freedom of choice of path, interpretation of text, and so on. Like all other religions, it is a given that Hindus see the purpose of life to be steering clear of evil and trying to achieve perfection. Hinduism allows that each individual is unique and as such not only can, but should pursue a path suited to that individuality. Perfectly complementing this abundance of individual expression is the multiplicity of forms in which the one true God can manifest. You are free to choose which of the thousands of manifestations of the Supreme Being will channel your worship. In fact, the major denominations of Hindus are based on which major manifestation of God is favored—Vaishnavas worshiping Vishnu, Shaivites worshiping Shiva, Shaktas worshiping Shakti, and Smartas who favor all of the five or six major manifestations of the Supreme Being.

Let me clear up one of the most prevalent misconceptions about Hinduism. It is *not* an *idolatrous* religion. This is how most other cultures perceive Hinduism and this is why the monotheistic religions despise it (yes, unfortunately, those of us who belong to a religion that does not allow any imagery in our worship consider ourselves superior to the others). They seem to be hardwired into believing that if an image is involved in worship, it is idolatry. I myself believed for decades that Hindus worshiped hundreds, thousands of idols!

Nothing could be further from the truth. As I explained above, Hindus believe in one true God, but let me quote one far more qualified than I on this subject, the great Persian Muslim scholar of the eleventh century, Al-Biruni, who himself lived in India for several years: "The Hindus believe with regard to God that he is one, eternal, without beginning and end, acting by free-will, almighty, all-wise, living, giving life, ruling, preserving; one who in his sovereignty is unique, beyond all likeness and unlikeness, and that he does not resemble anything nor does anything resemble him." [(5.1)] If only Muslims *today* could regard Hindus in this light!

Hinduism postulates that there are four major wants in human life. The first two belong to the way of desire and the last two to the way of renunciation. Basically it is recognized that man has an instinctive and natural desire for pleasure and it is a perfectly legitimate path to pursue—as long as no harm comes to self or others. It is also recognized that there will come a time when pleasure alone will not satisfy the yearnings of the soul. Another path to pursue would be the path of success: the pursuit of worldly success, possessions, and power, again, never harming others. When this path leads to no complete fulfillment either, the way of renunciation presents itself. You can choose duty—working not for yourself but for others, or for the community. A life in the service of others is immensely rewarding but it does require dedication and sacrifice. Yet even this, ultimately, leaves us wanting more. As Huston Smith says in *The World's Religions,* Hinduism recognizes that what humans ultimately want is "infinite being, infinite awareness and infinite bliss…these goods within peoples' reach…People already possess them."

To unlock our potential, Hinduism postulates four paths to God: the way to God through knowledge, love, work, and yoga (physical and mental disciplines). All of this pursuit of perfection may require several lifetimes. This brings us to reincarnation. The concept of reincarnation first appeared in Brahmanic writings of around the ninth century BC. Prior to that, most religions supposed the human spirit or even the body traveled to the other world and even provided food and equipment for this journey in burial rituals. Starting with the Upanishads, various Hindu texts subsequently introduced the concept of reincarnation and even spelled out in great detail the state in which reincarnations would occur, depending on the bad deeds in the present life. In other words, what deeds would result in incarnation as an outcast, a leper, or even an animal. Potentially a powerful incentive to lead a moral life!

Personally, I find reincarnation a tough sell. Surely, if it is true, we should be reincarnations ourselves, and if we are, how come we are unaware of our previous lives? Or, if not us, how come not a single person has come forward and acknowledged such awareness? And if we are blissfully unaware of how bad or good we were in a previous life, what is the point of punishing or rewarding deeds in a previous life with a worse or better reincarnated life? I mean, really, I live a terribly evil life and am reincarnated as, say, a bug. What is the purpose? Is the bug suffering pangs of remorse? Is anyone? Where is the punishment? I must be missing something here. Mind you, Hinduism is not the only religion to present such somewhat unfathomable scenarios.

Of course, another way to look at it is to accept, say, that if you are born into a low class, it is because of transgressions in an earlier life, and that you should really accept it and live virtuously so you will be reborn into a higher class. But again, where is the incentive if the *future* you has no idea of the *previous* you, and therefore, *you* do not reap the rewards? Also, by implying acceptance of the cards you are dealt with, there is a great incentive to exploit the situation—take advantage of the less fortunate and perpetuate their plight.

Yet while Hinduism is indeed a complex religion, it is a very noble one. Unfortunately, like all religions established after it, it too was eventually hijacked with devastating results that persist even today—the caste system! It is true that Hindu scriptures speak of four major *classes* (not castes) in society. These are the Brahmins (keepers of the sacred texts, teachers, spiritual leaders), Kshatriyas (warriors, administrators, keepers of the peace), Vaishyas (businessmen and farmers), and Sudras (workers, artisans, service providers—basically all others). These classes had nothing to do with caste or discrimination but merely attempted to recognize and work with the major structural framework of society in the ancient world—a structure found in most contemporary civilizations at the time.

The caste system, however, went far beyond the citations of class in the Hindu scriptures. Take the above four classes of society, add a fifth, the untouchables, and then introduce jatis or subgroups, thousands of them, into which people are born, marry (marrying outside one's jati is forbidden), and die, and you have an idea of India's caste system. The original idea and organization of a people based on class may have had some practical use in fostering order in society, etc., though I suspect it may well have had more use for one class (the few) than another (the many). However, like most such systems, it has long outlived its "usefulness" and has probably held India back for the last several centuries. The enormous iniquity suffered by the *masses* as a result of the rigid caste system in India and wherever it is practiced is a blight on the Hindu religion that may not have created it but *did nothing to eradicate it,* and, indeed, allowed it to flourish and to fit neatly into its system of beliefs about reincarnation (certain deeds would result in reincarnation into certain lower castes). I strongly believe this is another case of religion yielding to expediency and failing to correct course even when the evil harbored became abundantly manifest. *From an atheist point of view, the caste system in India resolves into nothing but an elaborate framework of slavery.* This is my "how come" question on Hinduism!

It is to India's credit that its constitution bans the caste system, and the country has attempted to correct the situation by such means as reserving a certain number of parliamentary seats for certain castes, etc. But the system is so deeply rooted that it will take decades for it to disappear, if at all, just as in the case of racial prejudice in the United States where, 150 years after the Civil War, and decades after civil rights legislation and Affirmative Action programs, prejudice is far from being eradicated, and racism is still fairly rampant. The situation is much better, yes, but there is still a long way to go. In India, this is particularly evident where marriage outside your caste is concerned. Still, there is some progress, and one would hope that as the country steps into the new technological era, barriers will fall, and what is now not even a trickle of change will eventually become a flood, and the whole edifice of caste will crumble. About time, really, because Hinduism without its caste system could have been more of a liberating experience for mankind than it has been.

Before I leave Hinduism and India, let me also say a few words about another unfortunate custom that India and Hinduism embraced, and, unfortunately, as in the case of the caste system, allowed to become perverted in the extreme. I refer to the dowry system. The dowry is a practice as old as civilization itself. In its purest, and some would say, original form, the dowry was originally intended to help a newly formed family establish itself and to provide for them in the event of the husband's death. It is a way of allowing the bride to carry her own weight, so to speak, in the marriage. As such, I envision it as an expression of the equality of the partners in a marriage, not as it has become patently obvious in too many Indian marriages—as an expression of the opposite. The dowry in India is all too often viewed as a payment to the groom's family (not to the coffers of the marriage) for the privilege of having your daughter marry their son. What nonsense! What a perversion! This view of the dowry automatically taints the bride as inferior and marks the groom as having to accept a person less than desirable. This practice is as insidious as the caste system and it transcends religion. Most families in India practice it regardless of their religion. This is another clear case, in my opinion, of religion failing to establish and retain higher moral ground when it should have. Another example of how moral progress, if it is to come, will do so from reason and not religion since it is man, not God, that perverts religion in the first place. Imagine the number of Indian families that have gone bankrupt amassing the dowry for their daughters! Or imagine the number of brides murdered because they were only married for their dowry or because their dowry was considered insufficient! I am confident, however, that the new generations of young, educated, and highly intelligent modern Indians are becoming ever more aware of these anachronisms, to put it mildly, and have already bravely started correcting them in increasing numbers.

Buddhism

Ah! Here is a religion that eschews violence in all its forms. It is even devoid of absolute imperatives. There are no commandments obliging you to adhere to a particular law of God or else be damned to a dire fate! The closest that Buddhism comes to commanding one's behavior are the five precepts:

1. Abstain from killing living beings—There's that nonviolence again. Put another way, this precept says simply: act with love toward all.
2. Abstain from taking what is not given—A milder version of "Thou shall not steal."
3. Abstain from sexual misconduct—The equivalent of the sixth commandment, but more sensible and far reaching.
4. Abstain from false speech.
5. Abstain from distilled substances that confuse the mind.

Simple aren't they? Yet profound! As you can see, Buddhism is more a way of life than a brotherhood, more culture than cult. All religions, really, have evolved into a set of guidelines on how to live your life, and it is here that they fail: while the world around us changes, religion steadfastly remains unchanged. The way we live changes, but the way religion tells us to live does not. Sometimes, worse still, religion changes the way we live our lives while the world around has not changed—this was the case leading up to the Reformation. The church became too intrusive in day-to-day life for no natural reason. Religion is intrinsically dogmatic, whether expressed or implied, and is therefore slow or unable to respond. This results in enormous pressure and the tearing apart of whole societies, some more peaceful than others. Much like earthquakes, caused when the pressure of opposing tectonic plates overcomes their resistance.

Buddhism is more laid-back and is not tied to dogma. It first describes and explains life and our very being as they are in terms easily recognizable (with birth starts a life that brings suffering, and, eventually, old age, sickness, and death) and then offers you a choice of how to live that life and redeem that being. In Buddhism, all sentient beings seek pleasure and avoid pain, and in so doing, they set themselves up for disappointment, dissatisfaction, and suffering. This carries over from one life to another (yes, they believe in reincarnation too), and the only way to break the cycle is to achieve enlightenment, which is found when all craving is eliminated.

This freedom from craving can be attained by following the teaching and path laid out by the Buddha and his followers. This is summarized by the Four Noble Truths of Buddhism: (a) life ultimately leads to suffering, (b) suffering is caused by craving, (c) suffering ends when true Nirvana and enlightenment end craving, and (d) enlightenment is attained by following the path laid out by Buddha.

That's it. Buddhism in a nutshell! Of all the religions I unfortunately do not know enough of, this is one I regret not getting to understand better. But it is clear that Buddhism is all about freeing ourselves from ignorance, craving, and delusions, and therefore, suffering, or quite simply, achieving Nirvana, which is the cessation of craving and the ending of the cycle of endless rebirths. It is more about being at peace with yourself than with God.

Buddhism was founded by Siddhartha Gautama, the son of a king in the sixth century BCE, who soon tired of the emptiness he was left with by his worldly, sumptuous lifestyle and went out into the world to seek fulfillment and meaning. It advocates a middle way of life as opposed to extreme indulgence on the one hand, and extreme mortification on the other. Note that Buddhism does not recognize an immortal soul as a distinct human attribute—an entity for each individual human being as the monotheistic religions and even Hinduism does.

I must say I find the Buddhist concept of rebirth and man's potentially many lives somewhat confusing. Even explanations from Buddhists themselves are unsatisfactory, and I feel here that Buddhists, like any other religious practitioners, do not fully understand their own religion, perhaps because it has gaps that have never been fully explained either by its founder or his disciples. I can accept that they do not believe in a soul as others do, namely that it is an entity by itself (my soul is a different entity from your soul), that it only inhabits the human body temporarily, and that it is free to exist by itself without a body in another place (heaven or hell) after death. I can understand them not believing this nor in the eternity of the soul, and in fact not believing in eternity itself, for anyone, even for the gods. But surely, if you believe that we are living beings, each separate from the others, that can be reborn almost endlessly, and indeed inhabit any one of a number of "planes" in those rebirths (including hell and the realms of the gods and demigods), then you must believe in *something* that transcends the human body and is capable of being reincarnated in another form in another life as a distinct entity, but in Buddhism, this "something" is not a distinct entity or soul or consciousness, it is more like "karmic energy" that reconstitutes in another life-form after death, and can, at some point in the cycle, dissolve into nothingness. Rather than placing emphasis on immortality and an individual soul, Buddhists believe that all beings are part of a single, transcending universe and go through a cycle of rebirths. These rebirths are determined by the laws of cause and effect (karma). Karma postulates that the intent behind every action, deliberate or implied, is a cause that has an effect. The effect can be either in this life or the next. As I said earlier, I am no expert, but I don't believe anyone is. I guess Buddhism allows each individual to attain his or her own comfort level in understanding the significance of being.

I hope I will not offend too many when I say that to my way of thinking, Buddhism is as close to atheism as you can get in a religion. The emphasis is placed on man—we are in control of our own destinies. There is no personal God or demon causing or contributing to our condition, and our actions affect not only our own lives but those of other men and creatures around us and those of future generations! There is a clear and brilliant concept of right and wrong and an unequivocal distinction between what is moral and immoral without the extremes that dogmatic religions go to. For instance, while adultery is expressly considered wrong, sex outside marriage and homosexuality do not have the same stigma, as long as no harm is involved, physical or psychological. Extreme and violent forms of punishment are also rejected such as capital punishment and severe physical punishment (cutting off the arms for stealing, torture, et cetera). Buddhism is an explicitly nonviolent religion in practice as well as in preaching.

Yet it is on this note, alas, that I must state my most serious misgiving about Buddhism, my "how come" dilemma. Despite Buddhism's obvious and amazing pedigree of pacifism, those societies that are predominantly Buddhist have had some of the most lamentable and atrocious records in human violence and exploitation. China, Japan, Myanmar, Cambodia, Vietnam, and North Korea, to name just some of them, in the last century alone, have witnessed waves of unspeakable violations of human rights and human dignity including mass murder rivaling that of the Nazis and Soviets. What does this tell us? That while the worst religious-inspired sentiment can fan the flames of hatred and evil into infernos, even the most peaceful religious sentiment cannot prevent the fires that man can kindle nor put out those fires once started; that while religion has been the direct cause of much grief, it has proved fairly ineffective in averting human tragedy when confronted with it; that even today, as it did eons ago, religion serves mainly to assuage our fears and ignorance at an individual level but is not terribly good at either enforcing collective moral behavior among peoples or preventing collective immoral catastrophes; and that perhaps in the case of Buddhism, nonviolence is translated as weakness and inability to control evil, so you are damned if you do and damned if you don't. In short, religion is failing one of its raisons d'être—to reign in out-of-control societies.

Judaism

While there are many other fascinating religions that merit consideration, with more followers than Judaism, I must resist the temptation to explore them in this book. There are far too many of them, it is not what this book is about, and quite frankly, as an atheist, and not being a philosopher, I find it difficult to be fully impartial, let alone fully understand the nuances of all the religions. I cannot, however, omit a section devoted to one of the oldest and most consequential religions. Over half of the world's population of close to 7 billion souls believe in the Jewish bible in one way or another and worship the God of Abraham and Moses. People who call themselves Jews, however, numbered just 13.4 million in 2010 according to the North American Jewish Data Bank.

Throughout history, the number of Jews has always been fairly inconsequential when you think about it, but there was a slim chance of Judaism itself being inconsequential given the enormous transformational change in philosophy it brought with it, and no chance at all when Christianity arose out of it some two thousand years ago. More specifically, neither Judaism nor Christianity would have had such a tremendous impact on world history and culture without what could arguably be called the most significant event in both religions: the "conversion" to Christianity of the Roman Emperor Constantine the Great! Up to that point, Christianity was basically a proscribed religion in the Roman Empire and the victim of many horrible persecutions starting with Nero's rule in 64 CE. By the time of Constantine's death in 337 CE, not only had he united the Roman Empire under one emperor, but by openly embracing Christianity, he made it a Christian empire at that. From this point on, the future of Christianity was assured, and, with it, Judaism itself. Without Christianity and without Rome's embracing it, would Judaism have endured and prospered as much as it has? Monotheism and its consequences could well have developed along other lines at other points in our history, perhaps even borrowing from a less influential Judaism. In fact, as stated earlier, Hinduism postulates only one almighty God. That Judaism survived, though, is not only because it spawned Christianity and Islam, which have been so successful, but to an equally significant extent to the awesome fortitude and perseverance of the Jewish people—the "Jewish nation" who survived against all odds. In fact, the very survival of the Jewish "nation" is considered by many a miracle itself.

I believe that central to this refusal to fade away despite all odds is the concept of "chosenness." As the Bible puts it: "For you are a holy people to Yahweh your God, and God has chosen you to be his treasured people from all the nations that are on the face of the earth." In its most generous interpretation this is taken to mean, as today's Reform Jews believe, the Jewish people have a covenant with God to bear witness to him and establish his justice and peace on earth. Over the millennia, it has imbued the Jews with a sense of obligation to do just that—bear witness—and to accept full responsibility for failure. "You only have I singled out of all the families of the earth: therefore will I visit upon you all your iniquities" (Amos 3:2).

Judaism has no central dogma or creed and no central infallible authority. Its teachings are to be found in its scriptures and sacred texts, the main ones being the Tanakh (Hebrew bible) and the Talmud. The Tanakh consists of three books, the first of which, the Torah, is subdivided into five books accepted by Christianity as the Old Testament (Genesis, Exodus, Leviticus, Numbers, and Deuteronomy). The Torah is believed to have been given to Moses on Mount Sinai though some biblical scholars dispute this and see no signs of Moses's authorship. But it appears to have been written probably in the fifth century BC as a compendium of separate texts from much earlier, starting in 900 BC. Scholars consider these time lines open to debate. Whatever the case, there is, as I stated, no central creed or dogma: the practice of Judaism is more a set of religious-cultural traditions and celebrations, and the scripture is interpreted within several degrees of latitude among different denominations, different rabbis, and even individual Jews. Prior to the breakup of the Jewish nation in AD 70, the Jewish faith was more structured in its public manifestation like other religions before and since, with priests in temples administering to the needs of the faithful and being the principal guardians and sources of interpretation of the texts. During this earlier period, besides kings and priests, a distinguishing feature of Judaism was, clearly, their prophets.

Prophets are a significant presence in Judaism. One encounters them in other cultures and religions too, but to a much lesser extent. In Judaism, they have a unique mission: as agents of change and as watchdogs. Where else in ancient times could a man dare to call attention to his ruler, admonish him for breaking God's law, and demand atonement? When the people stray too far from the righteous path and descend into depravity and sin a prophet invariably arises to set them straight. They were God's messengers sent to his beloved people to guide them and "touch base" with them—much like shepherds intervening periodically to protect and guide the flock.

After the dissolution of the Jewish nation, when the Diaspora resulted in the spreading of the Jewish community to the far corners of the world, it fell to the rabbis to preserve and continue the Jewish traditions and texts and culture and become the repositories of the faith, interpreting the sacred scripture. The Talmud commits to writing the rabbinic discussions on Judaism during this period, particularly Jewish law and ethics. Its two main parts, the Mishnah and Gemara, date from around 200 and 500 CE respectively.

Since any attempt to formalize Jewish beliefs into a creed by its most respected scholars and spiritual leaders has been met with rejection and criticism in the past, it is with great humility and trepidation that I summarize what I believe are some of Judaism's core tenets:

1. Belief in one and only one God who is incorporate, creator of all things, and omniscient—who knows all the deeds of man and will reward the good and punish the bad.

2. Belief that the Torah has not changed since it was given to Moses, and the words of the prophets are true.
3. Belief in the immortal soul, the coming of the Messiah, and the resurrection of the dead.
4. Belief in the covenant between God and the Jewish people.

Judaism is a way of life steeped in tradition, as witnessed by their religious holidays, some of which commemorate their "historical" events like Passover (the exodus from Egypt), Shavuot (the giving of the Torah on Mount Sinai), and Sukkoth (forty years wandering through the desert). No matter where in the world they are, their traditional prayers and daily blessings keep them united by referring repeatedly to their origin from and eventual return to their promised land, Israel. Their deep connection to the land of Israel is reminiscent of the strong ties of Muslims the world over to Medina and Mecca in what is today Saudi Arabia.

Oh sure, Jews have the same commandments as Christians do. (Or should that be the other way around?) Adultery is clearly forbidden and was even punishable by death in the Old Testament, but while orthodox Jewish law can be quite harsh, even today, the really savage punishments—death by stoning, burning, beheading, and strangulation—have hardly been applied for millennia. Just by observing Jewish acquaintances around me, and judging from what I can see in the media, I am inclined to believe that Judaism, particularly reformed and reconstructionist Jews, are extremely modern in outlook and totally against doctrinaire intrusions into their daily lives. They each observe the Jewish holidays and traditions and otherwise live their lives as they believe they should, much like each Hindu choosing the manifestation of God that most appeals to him/her and living his/her own version of the faith. Not surprisingly, Jews reputedly even have the largest percentage of atheists among religious groups—an estimated whopping 16 percent!

But towering over all else, Judaism's greatest contribution must surely be monotheism in its purest form—the belief in one and only one God who is supreme and personal and that man is created in

God's image, his supreme creation. It has been said that from this core belief has flowed a whole series of others that has proved transformational in Western philosophy. It is further said that Judeo-Christian influence accounts for one-third of Western civilization. This is obvious, particularly in ethics and morality, given that Christianity includes in its repertoire all the Jewish teachings from biblical times, and Christianity has dominated Western civilization since the late Roman period. It is, however, the humble opinion of this writer that the label Judeo-Christian is used too exclusively to describe Western civilization. A more appropriate description of Western civilization would be Greco-Roman-Judeo-Christian. There is little doubt that the Greco-Roman world played a seminal role in the development of the philosophy, laws, languages, arts, science, literature, government, and infrastructure, including city planning and civil engineering of the Western world, and Christianity itself evolved a Greco-Roman character. This being said, it is no secret that biblical stories are known and loved universally and have been a source of moral and ethical guidance throughout the ages, thanks, again, to the spread of Christianity with its Jewish heritage throughout most of the world either by conquest or missionary zeal.

To conclude this brief description of Judaism, I unfortunately have my "how come" question. Given that Judaism claims to be the religion that bears witness before all mankind to the highest standards of ethics and morality demanded by their one true God, how come the Jewish people are blind to the injustice that they have inflicted and continue to inflict on the Palestinians, having recently been victims of massive injustice themselves? How come they are willing to back up and defend their actions by acquiring the most horrific and destructive weapons the world has ever seen? How often will religion incite us to follow our beliefs and wind up with an almighty mess? Is this the will of God?

End Notes

(5.1) History of India; Edited by A. V. Williams Jackson, Ph.D., LL.D., Professor of Indo-Iranian Languages in Columbia University; Volume 9—Historic Accounts of India by Foreign Travellers Classic, Oriental, and Occidental; Chapter 4—Al-Biruni's Arabic Account of the Hindu Religion http://www.ibiblio.org/britishraj/Jackson9/chapter04.html

CHAPTER 6

DECONSTRUCTING GOD

The solution often turns out more beautiful than the puzzle

—Richard Dawkins

Now that we have surveyed the breathtaking story of the universe and our place in it and in the process demolished (or dismantled, to put it more mildly) the concept of a personal God and having established that in today's world religion is irrelevant (to put it bluntly) and indeed counterproductive, we should turn our thoughts to how we extricate ourselves from such deeply rooted habits. The change is so great that the being that emerges afterward will almost be another species. Or so it would seem. After all, man and religion have been inseparable forever.

As far as *Homo sapiens* is concerned, I believe religion and a belief in the supernatural were inherited mores. I have postulated earlier in this book that religion did not just start with our species but was part of the lives of the ancestors of *Homo sapiens,* or, at the very least, of our cousins. It is part and parcel of our psychological DNA, transmitted by "memes," to borrow from Richard Dawkins. Many fear that weaning ourselves off it will be tantamount to an enormous evolutionary change in our species. The withdrawal process could be catastrophic. To dissuade us from remotely considering such an option, visions arise of immorality and depravity, of a world in chaos. I have no idea why this is because there have been societies in the past, and certainly today, that belie this fear. China is largely an a-religious society and yet flourishes as highly civilized. But the fear of such radical change lingers and will be vigorously exploited to thwart efforts at DECONSTRUCTION.

So why undertake such an ordeal? Because we are at a stage in our evolution where religion has served its useful purpose and the point of diminishing returns has been reached and is well-passed; because it is better to control the process than wait for it to develop in an unwelcome manner; because enough is enough. Just because! The world has gone global and its seven-plus billion people live in instant proximity to each other. They are ever more interrelated and interdependent. In this environment, mutual understanding and a minimum of irritants are essential for the well-being of all. Religion is at best superfluous, at worst a very dangerous irritant. The sooner we come to terms with this situation, the better we shall face the future that awaits mankind.

Yet deconstructing religion and God will not be as fearsome as it sounds. In fact, since the dawn of time, the most enlightened thinkers and philosophers have always questioned the premise of God and religion. The essence of man's intelligence combined with his free will guaranteed that from the very start there were disbelievers. Atheism is as old as theism. It just did not catch on as theism did for reasons explained in earlier chapters—for one thing, it left far too many questions unanswered, questions that could not then be answered satisfactorily. Around the sixth and fifth centuries BC, atheist philosophical thought took hold in ancient Europe and Asia. Buddhism, in its inception, did not require worship of any particular deity, and is still, largely, a godless, albeit a very spiritual "religion." It is in fact more a way of life than a religion. Atheism was pushed by Greek philosophers starting as early as the sixth century BC when they attempted to come up with natural explanations for phenomena like lightning. It continued throughout Greek history, though accusations of atheism were often politically motivated. And it has continued throughout world history. In countries like China and Japan, religion and God were never as dogmatic and transcendental as in other regions. What they valued above all else was culture itself: rules to live by and models to foment civilization. In most of the rest of the world, however, it was not healthy to be atheist.

During the Renaissance (late thirteenth through early seventeenth centuries), and particularly the Reformation (sixteenth through seventeenth centuries), criticism of religion became more open and schisms appeared in Christian Europe, but it was not till the Enlightenment, in the eighteenth century, that atheism finally emerged into the open. In the late 1770s, the French Revolution provided a significant impetus. The open discourse on the subject during that period was patronized by notables such as Jean-Jacques Rousseau, David Hume, Adam Smith, and Benjamin Franklin. In America, John Adams and Thomas Paine were deists (did not believe in a personal God), as was Benjamin Franklin. Thomas Jefferson was totally turned off by the superstitious nature of Christianity. In writing to Peter Carr in 1787 he says:

> Fix reason firmly in her seat, and call to her tribunal every fact, every opinion. Question with boldness even the existence of a God; because, if there be one, he must more approve of the homage of reason, than that of blindfolded fear. Do not be frightened from this inquiry by any fear of its consequences. If it ends in a belief that there is no God, you will find incitements to virtue in the comfort and pleasantness you feel in its exercise, and in the love of others which it will procure for you.[6.1]

In a letter to Dr. Benjamin Rush, dated April 21, 1803, he says: "I am a Christian, in the only sense in which he [i.e. Jesus] wished anyone to be: sincerely attached to his doctrines in preference to all others, ascribing to himself every *human* excellence, and believing he never claimed any other" (6.2) (The clarification in brackets and italics are mine). Does this not imply that he did not believe in the divinity of Jesus? And when he wrote what has become known as the Jefferson Bible, he was well into deconstruction. In it he attempts to separate the ethical teachings of Jesus contained in the traditional Bible from the dogma and supernatural mumbo jumbo. He loved and espoused the morality of Jesus, the man, and he rejected the supernatural claims made by others about Jesus. As I have been saying, all the good we ascribe to God and all the morality preached by religion is none other than the good and morality in us, his creators! Jefferson deconstructed God and religion for himself, separating morality from mirage. It is time we do, too. Keep the morality, which was ours to begin with, and discard the confusing and dangerous mumbo jumbo!

Yes, we have indeed answered most of the questions our ancient forebears posed in ages past: questions about our origin, about our nature, and the physical world around us. Yet more questions than ever remain. But whereas in our early history religion and God were our comfort zones and buffered all our unanswered questions, today, rational men are comfortable and confident with science and secularism and accept that it is time to shed our old crutches as they no longer help—they hinder. Today, people realize that significant aspects and teachings of religion are more and more out of sync and out of touch with mankind's knowledge of the universe, with his own origins, and, moving forward, with his goals and vision, and have little, if any, application to the reality of the second millennium.

Deconstruction is when people first stop going to church. They soon become agnostics. Many will continue to identify as agnostics even though they no longer believe in the existence of any God, let alone a personal God. Read any poll on the subject and you will see that agnosticism is growing. Quite rapidly. Deconstruction is everywhere around us, already in motion, and is gathering momentum. It is, in my view, a natural outcome of cultural evolution. It is not a question of whether it will start, but how fast will it proceed, and when will it complete. Besides, by not publicly recognizing and aggressively pursuing deconstruction, at least as aggressively as some religions proselytize, there is a very real danger that a void will be created in which a large group of humanity will feel rudderless and could be susceptible to passivity or misguided ideologies—*a void that could result in totally undesirable consequences.*

One of the most glaring voids in modern human society is the absence of overt expressions of agnosticism and/or atheism. There are no political movements that openly embrace atheist principles and philosophy. There is no public media devoted to its propagation. We have TV channels that cater to religious factions, and we have many devoted to Hispanics (13 percent of the US population) and African Americans (also 13 percent). Where is the media in America for the 16 percent of the population that describe themselves as without religion, of which 6 to 9 percent say they are out and out atheists?

In the world's most powerful and free nation, the Constitution, in its First Amendment, clearly states that: "Congress shall make no law…abridging the freedom of speech, or of the press; or the right of the people peaceably to assemble." Yet agnostics and atheists do not assemble on the same scale as their religious brethren do. If they did, deconstruction would proceed at a much more acceptable pace. Why is this? In my humble opinion, it is fear—fear of public opinion or of being considered an outcast. And passivity. Passivity in failing to recognize the insidious nature of the negatives of religion and leaving it for time to take its course. Don't get me wrong! I know there are a number of books on atheism and the secular school of thought. There are some notable members of the entertainment world that openly present their atheist views on television programs. Atheists do meet across the country much like other myriads of associations. This is true, but these efforts are still insignificant compared to organized religion and the organization of religious factions in the press, media, and public service. Bishops and other religious leaders speak, and the world knows the church has spoken. Why, even African and Latin Americans have their spokespersons and ready access to the media. Who speaks for the atheists? How is our message being heard in the public forum? Does the world know us as we really are? Yes, deconstruction is proceeding apace, but the pace needs to be controlled, directed, and quickened.

It is true that in some parts of the world, religions are reporting *more* conversions. This is particularly true either in the less developed countries or where religious intolerance was recently lifted. But the trend in the developed countries is clearly away from established religion. Even in the USA, arguably the most religious of the advanced countries, this trend is apparent. The number of Americans claiming no religion at all doubled since 1990 to 16.1 percent in 2007 (of which 5.8 percent were "religious unaffiliated"). Another study, the American Religious Identification Survey (ARIS), shows a jump from 8.2 percent in 1990 to 15 percent in 2008 for the "None/No Religion" category, with most of the erosion coming from the Christian faiths. The CIA *World Factbook* shows that 80.8 percent of Vietnam still professes no religion despite the fact that religion is no longer forbidden or pressured. The same is true for the former Soviet states. After the complete lifting of the prohibition of religion, while some churchgoing has returned, there has been no rush to fill the pews.

Europe is a particularly interesting case study. Since the Enlightenment in the eighteenth century and with the advent of increasing secularization, Europe's religiosity was universally considered to be steadily declining. In the last few decades, even holdout Catholic countries like Italy, Spain, and Ireland have shown great declines in church attendance, with increasing percentages declaring themselves agnostic or atheist. This trend is reversed in some of the Eastern Bloc countries like Poland where, I believe, a lot of the religiosity has to do with the role the church has played in their historic resistance to Soviet intrusion. The difference between western and eastern European countries also demonstrates the link between socioeconomic conditions and religiosity. The more well-off people are, or the more secure they feel in, say, a welfare state, the less they need religion and vice versa. However, the inevitable decline of religion in each country or region is not equal across all religions. Due mainly to immigration, the Islamic faith is increasing rapidly in Europe as is the Hindu population in the UK. Smaller denominations of the Christian faith are also doing quite well, such as the Evangelicals. The churchgoing trend, however, among the established mainstream faiths and denominations is decreasing, and I submit that as the other faiths and denominations have become "established" in a region, they, too, will start to decline. The overall rate of decline in some faiths will be extremely slow, to the point that at a given time, none is detected and in fact the opposite appears to be true.

Take the Taliban movement in Afghanistan. As of today, 2015, it appears not only to not be dead but making a comeback. My reply to that is yes, but look at the country and the society! What I see here is a society that is isolated, not openly exposed to modern knowledge, poor, and organized in an almost medieval tribal way, with half of its members, women, denied education and other basic rights—and above all, a corrupt society. In these circumstances, how can they not succumb to misguided doctrine and ideologies? In fact, it is truly admirable that they have come as far as they have.

All this places deconstruction of God and religion in focus. *Deconstruction is happening.* This has been going on for a long time. It is clearly gathering momentum and has been for decades past. However, we should not allow it to develop at its "natural" pace. There is too much at stake. For one thing, ATHEISM ITSELF COULD BE HIJACKED INTO SOME EXTREMIST FORM, if left rudderless and in a vacuum. While the prospect of a clash between Islam and the West cannot be discarded, there are other looming difficulties the world will face—the resolution of which should only be helped absent religious influences on policy. The problem is not so much how to deconstruct, but how to speed up the deconstruction. WE NEED TO *FACILITATE* DECONSTRUCTION. How do we go about this?

We could start by truly separating church and state in our own country. It should be made clear that morality is not, and never has been, a purely Christian or Judeo-Christian attribute, and in fact, morality is even more moral with the complete absence of religious influence. The claim of moral superiority by these groups is the single most repugnant offense in American public life. Let the religious standing of all public officials be discussed openly without fear of the religious discrimination or religious intolerance labels. We should particularly be active in helping elect those brave individuals who publicly assert their agnosticism or freedom from religious influence and are willing to test their morality against others. Perhaps this is terribly naive in a society where gays and lesbians can get elected, but, to my knowledge, no openly professed atheist has. Pete Stark was elected in 1972 and came out as an atheist in 2007. He was not returned in 2012. THERE ARE CURRENTLY NO OPENLY ATHEIST MEMBERS IN CONGRESS—by far, the least represented group of all (by the way, in Pete's case, forty years in congress was probably all the reason needed).

In this country, the cradle of Democracy, it is unthinkable that atheists are prohibited from holding public office in seven states: Arkansas, Maryland, Mississippi, North and South Carolina, Tennessee and Texas. Maybe it is just inertia and a reluctance to sponsor changes to such laws, but the effect is very real. In the past atheists have had to fight court battles to hold down their jobs.

On the other end of the spectrum there are thirteen countries where atheism is punishable by death: Afghanistan, Iran, Malaysia, Maldives, Mauritania, Nigeria, Pakistan, Qatar, Saudi Arabia, Somalia, Sudan, United Arab Emirates and Yemen. There are several other countries that punish blasphemy or apostasy with prison time or restrict a-religious speech and thought. Think about it: homo sapiens is still struggling to come to terms with its intellectual endowments. The darkness has not lifted the world over.

But this step alone, getting atheists elected, would go a long way in deconstruction. In other words, let us first get our house in order the way we want it before attempting to clean houses elsewhere. It will only take one openly atheist person to get elected to public office to open the gates for others. Not only will we be facilitating deconstruction, we will also ensure that atheism itself will evolve in a controlled, not rudderless way.

In fact ideally, we should never be the ones to clean houses elsewhere (other countries). This should be a local, spontaneous, self-induced movement in each country. We should only facilitate the efforts and could start by increasing our knowledge of other cultures and their knowledge of ours. The more world cultures are drawn into dialogue, contact, and instant access to each other, the more will it be apparent that, despite religious differences, there is more that we share in common than not. Instead of having a TV program showing our great missionary work in India and helping bring God to the heathens, we could have a program about a typical Hindu family showing their daily struggles and how they cope with them within a framework of morality and challenges not unlike ours. Show how much they really are like us. The more we become aware of our similarities, the more irrelevant will religious distinctions become.

At the very least, we should make every attempt to get to know the other side. Today, one such side is Islam. While the sensational side of a story gets aired ad infinitum, the more sober truth often never surfaces. Talk radio, or more appropriately, hate radio is quick to demonize all of Islam. This is a shame. Deconstructionists should not seek to demonize other religions and other cultures. They should constantly make the point that *no religion is inherently evil, but all religions are obsolete*, out of touch with modern man, and subject to abuse. What deconstructionists could do here is to spread the truth about the situation. It is clear that the jihadists are hijacking their faith and represent everything that can go wrong when certain conditions and situations are ignored. Remember, THE TERRORISTS ARE TERRORIZING ISLAM TOO. Perhaps what is happening is something akin to what happened in Germany. No rational person will believe that all Germans shared the loathsome goals the Nazis did. Indeed it is safe to assume that the majority did not. Yet no violent protests were forthcoming. The campaign of terror waged by the SS was an effective dampener in Germany, and the world was too weak and weary after the great war and the Great Depression to do much about it until they were forced to. This even applies to our country—forced to enter the fray only when Japan bombed Pearl Harbor.

God knows that during the years leading up to the Nazi horror there were plenty of warnings, yet the world stood by, not just helpless but, more importantly, clueless. The sorry state Germany found itself in after World War I provided a breeding ground for discontent that was exploited by a small band of crazed individuals who had come to believe that they were saviors who would restore their *superior* race and remove an offending one. If the world had poured the same help and effort into reconstructing Germany *then* that it did later, after World War II, the war itself would never have occurred, and what a different story that would have been! The Holocaust would not have happened, and Israel, if it happened at all, would not have come about the way it did, and Islamic terrorists would probably not have flourished and received as much support as they have.

There are a lot of similarities today. The situation in the Middle East is nothing if not a hotbed of discontent and opprobrium, yet for the past six decades, we have let it fester, with no bold solution in sight. In many ways, we, the American public, are just as clueless as we were about the rise of Nazism in Germany. Fitted with the blinkers of our religion and looking through Judeo-Christian tinted glasses, we do not see and understand the full reality of the situation from the Palestinian side or from the Sunni/Shia paradigm, and all our efforts are thus thwarted. All we see is their terrorism and our righteousness. Maybe we need a kind of Marshall Plan for the area, not just a plan of bricks and mortar but also to build bridges of understanding and to develop trading of ideas; and we need it now not after the worst has happened or after another six million have perished, this time in a nuclear, chemical, or biological holocaust, and perhaps not just on the banks of the Jordan, but also on the banks of the Hudson or the Potomac.

Imagine that when it comes to making major policy decisions every member of the executive and legislative branches is somehow magically incapable, try as hard as they can, of summoning their personal religious, ethnic, or cultural instincts to bear. That, try as hard as they can to fight it, they can only call on the highest rational, moral, impartial, and practical principles in formulating policy. What would those policies look like? Would we be in the sorry situation we are now in? The cynics among us would rush to point out that such talk is naive, ridiculous, and utopian, and they are probably right that unfortunately, such magic is impossible to come by. It is left to us to work as hard as we can to elect only those people who come closest to being free of such influences.

Unfortunately, our track record to date is just the opposite. Too often, it is a candidate's display and manipulation of religion that gets him elected. It is time to reverse this trend. We could do this by asking the candidates pointed questions involving religion. I know it has been taboo so far, but it is time for secularism to come out of the closet. We should clearly establish the ties between a legislator's religion and his legislation. Why exactly are you against abortion? Is it because God forbids it, because of the immortal soul, or because of specific scientific, moral, or rational reasons? Remember the inadvertent geography tests that Bush and Palin were subjected to? What if we not only ask specific questions about religious ideology of our candidates to get an idea of their religiosity and how it might affect their decisions but also about their knowledge of other religions, particularly Islam? Since Islam is the recruiting ground for the current terrorist groups, should we not have more than a completely biased understanding of it and see that it, too, is a victim? That we need to be working *with* Islam instead of against it? AND WE SHOULD DO ALL THIS IN THE PRIMARY ELECTIONS. Initially, such an approach will backfire and get even more orthodox believers elected. So be it. Ah, therein lies the rub. See what a steep hill to climb, and what a wonderful opportunity too? I write elsewhere on the unfortunate glitches I see in our electoral system. But it is what it is.

Once a candidate is elected at the primary level, it may be too late. If you are Republican and atheist and a very religious person gets the Republican nomination in the primaries, will you vote for the Democrat in the general election (assuming he is not as dangerously religious)? Much better to have elected a better candidate in the primary, but remember, the primaries have a pitiful turnout, so if the atheists identify their candidates of choice and wage a major drive to get out their vote, we will have made huge progress.

Hopefully it will not be long before the pendulum will swing in the other direction, and we will start to see a true separation of church not so much from state, which the Constitution ensures anyway, but from legislation—a separation of the pulpit from public policy, where its intrusion is far too insidious. The $64,000 question to put to our presidential contenders is this: Do you believe that our problems cannot be solved without God intervening? Above all, we need the media to present a-religious viewpoints more openly and to expose clearly religious motivations in public policy. *We need atheists to step up and stake out the higher moral ground!*

We could also help speed up the economic and social development of the poorer countries. The more developed a society is, the less poverty there is, and the less dependence on the spurious comforts of religion. The more this happens, the more will religions have to adapt to modern circumstances. The more they do, the more credibility they lose. If they do not adapt, they will also lose relevance and, therefore, credibility. It's a lose-lose situation for them. Agnostics may believe in God, but this belief takes on a whole new meaning without the restrictions of religion. Over time, agnosticism may or may not turn to atheism. This is not the point. The point is to disallow religion to cloud purely secular issues and to allow for the innate human capacity to discern good from evil to flourish and inform world social, economic, and political affairs.

We should identify the regions where the need for modernization in outlook is greatest or where the social organization is most backward. This should not be too difficult. These will be the countries where women are held back from their full potential by being denied education, free access to all careers, discriminated against by the courts with particularly harsh and one-sided justice, and so on. Countries where human rights are most blatantly denied to not just individuals but whole classes of society like all women, all children, all members of a particular caste or tribe or, yes, religion too.

Once identified, we should pursue a policy to persuade the people to change with every legitimate means at our disposal. This should be done not just by ourselves in isolation, but on the world stage, enlisting the world community in the process. These regions may be insignificant in economic terms or not, but if we are to be a peaceful, moral world, every member should be brought into the fold, lest a situation like this could blossom into an unwelcome and serious problem later.

After all, we act on a global scale to geographically identify and deal with potentially global threatening situations like excessive carbon dioxide pollution that causes global warming, or areas where, say, a disease like smallpox threatens a comeback. What about regions where there are major departures from basic human morality and situations that pose a threat to slow or even stop the enlightened and emancipated advance into our future? We ignore them at our peril!

Again, the only way I know to hasten deconstruction is to push our agenda—at every opportunity, at every turn. And I don't mean some hidden, malicious agenda, I mean, quite simply, our agenda to ensure that politics is in no way, shape, or form a reflection of a particular religion's doctrine but the result of purely rational processes. For instance, abortion. If there is no God, it is not a sin against God and should not be banned for that reason. The law stating the circumstances where abortion is disallowed should be based on a reasoned consensus among us as to when a fetus should be considered a person and therefore endowed with human rights. From this point on, abortion should be considered akin to murder and should therefore be regulated. If we enlist the help of scientists, fine, if this enhances the prospects for the most reasoned decision. Our reasoning might include thresholds for such factors as health prospects of mother and fetus—if solid and acceptable reasoning is involved. There may be rational grounds where decisions have to be made as to who survives if only one can, etc. But to just say no to everybody based on religious doctrine? I have to balk at that. If a particular person refuses to abort because of religious convictions, fine. But that's as far as it should go. Your religious convictions do not give you the right to deny to another what society as a whole considers acceptable in certain circumstances, absent religious convictions. If your religion forbids blood transfusions, fine, but do not attempt to make blood transfusions illegal for everyone. The same goes for euthanasia. Let us allow it or not, based on legal and rational considerations, not on religious grounds.

What most people do not realize is that religion is purely a system of beliefs. No one would argue that it is all right to impose your system of beliefs on others—by law, forcefully. If society at large believes that abortion is acceptable in certain circumstances and passes laws to that effect, anti-abortion groups are free to state their opinions, but they cannot seek to forcibly prevent others from availing themselves of the law. You cannot force your system of beliefs on those who have reasonably debated and rejected them.

Some will now say, "So it is OK for women in certain African tribes to be sexually mutilated because this is in accordance with their traditions?" The answer is obviously no. On the one hand, we are talking about a conclusion reached after much open discussion and reasoning, including by the most respected scientists, and agreed to by all sexes; and on the other, we are talking about a practice that has been recognized as primitive every time it is openly discussed in free societies, that has been abolished by other societies, and is practically always enforced against the will of the victims in societies where the tradition is also to deny women a voice. The fact that they also happen to be mostly Muslim societies is incidental given that Islam not only does not mandate the practice but even condemns it (compare this to Hinduism not mandating the caste system but condoning it). As an aside, I submit that such mores are established more in a geographical area spanning one or more very similar *cultures,* and it is incidental that the *religion* prevailing in that area is what it is.

Apropos of deconstruction and FGM (female genital mutilation), it is becoming increasingly common now for people to refer to this practice as FGC (female genital cutting) because of the negative connotation that "mutilation" bestows. Aggressive deconstruction would insist on calling it mutilation and not cutting! While we should shy away from the shrill and strident language of, say, hate radio, we should never hesitate to be forthright in our denunciation of wrongdoing for what it is. We should be firm, consistent, and unwavering in our support of reason over superstition and outdated, unacceptable traditions. We should not hesitate to call a spade a spade. So let me clearly state that what ISIS is doing is BARBARIC, MEDIEVAL, EVIL, AND TOTALLY UNINFORMED!

Now just for the record, let us talk briefly about what atheism is and, more important, about what it is not. Atheism is not a turning away from God *to* the Devil. Atheism, as used in this book, denies not just the existence of God but also the Devil and of all things supernatural. For instance, a lot of very smart people confuse atheism with, or cannot distinguish it from demonism, Satanism, and such. A better definition, in my opinion, is that atheism is quite simply the belief in physical reality and a rejection of all things supernatural—good, bad, or indifferent.

As I stated earlier, since man created God *and* the Devil (Actually, man's forebears probably did; I'm sorry, I didn't state this earlier?), it follows that atheists believe that it is man who is capable of, or aspires to the sublime good that he attributes to God since they are attributes he conceived and longed for in the first place, and likewise, it is man who is capable of the evil attributed to the Devil. TO AN ATHEIST, THE BUCK STOPS WITH US. Do not praise God for good works—we are the ones who perform them and there's always room for more. Don't blame the Devil for evil—we and only we are responsible. And if the good works were not performed by man, let's be thankful for random luck, not God—for example, the weather behaved and provided an abundant crop or a disease remitted in an apparently spontaneous manner. God does not perform miraculous cures. The person miraculously cured of cancer was lucky he or she had a spontaneous recovery for reasons not yet discovered; and God did not send the rain—the rain was caused by a convergence of climatological variables. These things can, and do happen. Science does not have to have all the answers: there will always be some natural phenomena that we are as yet unable to explain or predict. Atheists are able to live with that. As the frontiers of our knowledge expand, more of these cases will be explained. By the same token, if a major hurricane strikes and causes untold suffering and destruction, do not blame it either on the Devil or the wrath of God. Discussing the devastating earthquake in Haiti in January 2010 that claimed hundreds of thousands of lives and untold destruction, here is what Pat Robertson had to say on his television show, and I quote:

"Something happened a long time ago in Haiti, and people might not want to talk about it. They were under the heel of the French, you know, Napoleon III, or whatever. And they got together and swore a pact to the Devil. They said, 'we will serve you if you will get us free from the French.' True story! And so, the Devil said, 'O.K. It's a deal.' And they kicked the French out. You know, the Haitians revolted and got themselves free. But ever since, they have been cursed by one thing after the other—-desperately poor. That island of Hispaniola is one island, cut down the middle. On one side is Haiti, on the other side is the Dominican Republic. The Dominican Republic is prosperous, healthy, full of resorts, et cetera.., Haiti is in desperate poverty. Same island! They need to have, and we need to pray for them, a great turning to God."[(6.3)]

Now Pat Robertson has been an important leader of the religious right for decades. Besides numerous TV and radio shows, his *700 Club* television program has been active since 1966 and has a television daily audience of one million viewers. Why, he even was a Republican presidential candidate in 1988! Not only is he influential but he has the ear of many influential people. Thank God he lost his presidential bid!

On September 11, 2001, Islamist terrorists struck, destroying the World Trade Center towers in New York, part of the Pentagon in DC, and crashing a United Airlines flight in Pennsylvania, resulting in 2,996 deaths including the nineteen hijackers. Two days later in the same *700 Club* show, on September 13, Pat Robertson and guest, Jerry Falwell, an ordained Baptist minister and leader of the religious right, managed to convey that God lifted the curtain and allowed the enemies of America to give us "probably what we deserve." He assigned God's wrath to the ACLU for their role, with the public courts system, in throwing God out of the public square and out of the schools, and the abortionists for their role in destroying 40 million innocent babies. In short, he went on to say, and I quote:

"The paganists, and the abortionists, and the feminists, the gays and the lesbians..., the ACLU, People for the American Way, all of them who tried to secularize America, I point the finger in their face and say, 'You helped this happen.'"[(6.4)]

Really? This was the man who founded the moral majority, for Pete's sake! In case you have forgotten, the moral majority was founded in 1979 and dissolved in the late '80s. It was very active in the elections of 1980, 1984, and 1988, supporting the Republicans in every one of them (Reagan and George H. W. Bush). A man who thinks the way Jerry does easily goes to the next step and identifies God's enemies and the need to wage war against them. You have to believe a goodly portion of his supporters would cheer this on. I mean, why else would they support him?

I could devote a chapter to the inanities spoken and acted out in the name of religion just in our country—forget the world—but I have already said that this is really not my purpose. Let me just use the above to point out why it is imperative that we keep the Robertsons and Falwells and all their adherents out of government. *Keep any fervently religious person out of politics*! *If they are so religious, they do not have or will not spend the time and effort to find the most reasoned secular solutions we deserve*! They will be inclined to pray to, listen to, and actually take guidance from God! And God *will* speak to them, but it will be their subconscious telling them what their misguided minds want to hear! They are welcome to pray all they want. But we do not want doctrine, dogma and, indeed, superstition akin to the very paganism they decry to influence government. Let us instead keep our heads and use reason, intelligence, and pragmatism to provide our solutions and shape our destiny. *They are free to run for office, but it is up to us to stop them from being elected, and shame on us if we do not vote, especially in the primaries.*

That brings me to this: atheists and agnostics, particularly, should do all they can to get full participation in the electoral system. Nothing dismays me more than to see poor participation in the elections. God knows (force of habit) we are burdened with one of the most absurd electoral systems in the free world. This, perhaps, is the price you pay for being the first democracy—the newer ones learn from our experience. I was shocked to learn recently that there are, if I remember correctly, twenty-two countries, no, make that twenty-one (North Korea excluded, ha!) and a canton in Switzerland where voting is obligatory (but enforced in only nine of them). Shouldn't we do our utmost to encourage full participation, like making voting day a holiday? More and more people work two jobs, for instance, and are unlikely to vote. Shouldn't we make it really easy to vote early, and yes, if we do all of that we could then justifiably make it obligatory and punishable if not performed.

As I said, we are burdened with (a) a system of primaries where those candidates catering to the extremes of their parties are the most likely to get elected; (b) a system of midterm elections which also draws mostly a minority hardcore group of electors; (c) a senate which has become too misrepresentative, where a large number of seats are assigned to a relatively small percentage of the population, larger, I am sure, than was envisaged by the founders; and (d) a legislative/executive setup that all too frequently results in a dysfunctional government like we keep having all too frequently, not to mention the election calendar where we can renew the presidency every four years but the congress every two years, and the six-year senate terms can only be renewed one-third at a time—every two years. Kind of messy, don't you think? I see nothing but built-in instability. Some of it may have made sense in the early days of our nation, when new states and territory were being added and the different local economies and subcultures established. But today is not the late eighteenth or early nineteenth centuries! Add to this the fact that in today's world, what happens to our economy and security is very much dependent on events beyond our control in other parts of the world, and you have a recipe for chaos and, yes, gridlock. And overriding all of this is the perception shared by many that the Constitution is not a living document and should not be tampered with. I have no doubt that our founding fathers are turning in their graves!

But I digress again. The important thing to remember is that to the atheist, one neither praises nor blames God or the Devil for anything. Man's destiny is in his hands and his hands alone. This is the way most rational men think, including agnostics and your average believer too. All things being equal, the atheist activist will always look to maximize good and minimize evil—more so than the religious activist (the religious activist who thinks evil is God's retribution will be more likely to accept it than fight it). The atheist is not going to sit around and wait for supernatural intervention. Besides, the actions of the atheist will be more transparent and, therefore, more effectively dealt with. If the desired results are not achieved, new action will be forthcoming and changes can be made. Atheists are not bound by the inflexibility of dogma or the infallibility of faith. The religious activist, on the other hand, sets out to do what he sees is good even if this is evil for others and it is not easy to deal with this—even if it is transparent (not always the case). How do you deal with faith? How do you revise dogma?

The Palestinian situation is a good example. Hey, do not get mad at me for harping on the Palestinian situation. The Soviet threat has gone (OK, as I revise my book, Putin has become an unbearable and dangerous element), China is now our largest trading partner, Vietnam, Cambodia, etc. are history, Osama bin Laden is dead, but as long as I can remember, since I was eight years old, Palestine has been a constant in the headlines! Anyway, the West was clearly maximizing good and minimizing evil for the Jews when they created the modern Palestine—if you look at it on ethno-religious grounds. But they actually maximized evil and minimized good for the Palestinians, and it has been impossible to redress the situation since. I can assure you that if the West were atheist at the time, a solution far more acceptable to all parties would have been found—not without pain, mind you, but more equitable all around. And if the Palestinians were also atheists, I suspect that an even less painful solution would have resulted. Before you rush to point out that the Zionist movement was not a religious movement but was actually founded by secular Jews to create a state and a homeland to preserve their *cultural* identity, allow me to state my belief that many "cultures" are primarily anchored in religious teachings and the Jewish culture is no exception. The ethno-religious culture of the Jews identifies Israel as their promised land—a promise made to Moses by their God. There is scarcely a Jew the world over that does not at some point in his or her week, month, or year, pray for, wish for, and, in many cases, actively support a favorable outcome for the Jewish state of Israel.

The above argument is similar to the conflict between Shiites and Sunnis in Iraq. There are those who insist it is purely secular—a struggle for sharing of oil resources, a struggle for power. To those people I pose the question: If both factions were of the same religious sect, say, all Sunni or all Shiite, would there be any struggle at all, and if there were, would it be so virulent and unsolvable? Is not the main antagonism between Shiite and Sunni based on intra-religious bickering dating all the way back to the succession of the prophet Muhammad?

So let it be clear, the absence of religion and God, far from throwing us into a spiral of increasing amorality, would rid us of much strife and conflict and bring a higher morality to the world. I cannot repeat often enough: since God and religion are creations of man, all the morality that stems from them really is man's doing. If the *created* is moral, it stands to reason that the *creator* knows about morality. By the same token, if the created is evil, the creator unfortunately knows evil too. Ask any novelist and he will tell you that the better novels are based on fact and the best ones are autobiographical. God and the Devil are the fictional characters forged in man's autobiographical psyche! Why should morality stop? Why should it not be improved, instead, to reflect man's current station along evolution's path? Why should the battle against evil stop? Fighting evil will be more effective by bringing the battlefield down to earth where it belongs!

Take law and order as the most obvious manifestation of morality and moral principles. Remember, atheists are ordinary people, and like all people, they realize that law and order are necessary for human peace, progress, and survival. Their implementation of law and order will reflect their belief that all good and all evil is our and only our responsibility. Unlike religious people, however, their law and order will not be tainted with religious undertones. They will not impose punishments outlined in ancient and obscure scriptures that have clearly outlived their relevance. An atheist's morality is universal, not sectarian, so neither will his laws be sectarian. It is also, yes, updateable, not mired in a time warp.

Unfortunately for the atheist, the prospect does not appear to brighten any when you contemplate recent so-called godless societies. Most recent examples would be the Soviet Union and its Eastern European communist allies. It should be noted, though, that the dismal record of these countries is attributable to their Marxist totalitarian philosophy and not to atheism, just as the record of the Fascist regimes in Germany and Italy is attributable entirely to their sociopolitical agenda rather than the religion professed by their members. Hitler was in fact Catholic but his views about religion ranged all over the spectrum including that God had chosen the Aryan race to excel above all others. While many Jews are bitter about the church's inability at the time to turn back the Nazi tide, no rational person can blame religion for the evil that ensued. By the same token, atheism per se did not cause the evil of the Soviet Union. If any conclusion can be drawn from these examples, it is that evil, clearly, arises irrespective of whether religion is present or not, because as I will never tire saying, good and evil have nothing to do with God and the Devil but everything to do with the nature of man.

Since the Soviet Union dissolved, atheism is less of a force in Russia than before, and religiosity, though far less than in the West, is far greater than in the Soviet era. Despite that fact, Russia has not been faring too well. To hear some people put it, corruption, crime, and greed reign supreme with no end in sight. Before dissolution, the Soviet Union was a totalitarian state guilty of atrocities that, in total numbers, are reputed to have surpassed even the Holocaust—and by multiples! No, atheism did not cause it, totalitarianism did. Man's inhumanity to man did. Again, incontrovertible proof that evil must be laid at man's door not the Devil's, not religion's and, indeed, not atheism's doors. I assume it is abundantly clear to my readers by now that the buck stops with us. Deconstructing God entails jealously guarding and strengthening our moral compass.

Let me make it clearer still. For the purposes of this book, I use the word atheism in its purest sense—without God. It refers to situations where God is left out of the picture altogether. Of course, this also implies that religion is out too. Atheism lays the responsibility for our affairs directly at our doorstep. It implies that all good and all evil are none other than man's doing. It is therefore up to man to decide which will prevail. This struggle will continue as it always has, but will occur in a different arena where good and evil are not viewed through the polarized lenses of religion but in their absolute terms, as products of man's free will. We will continue to do battle against evil, but it will be on our terms and under our control.

Before I move on, let me address a question that always comes up. Will evil not increase in a world without God and religion? An excellent question. In most religions, the afterlife prospects are designed to induce good behavior in this life. Absent these prospects, what incentive is there to not steal, murder, commit adultery, and generally live the good life at the expense of others? This may sound like the showstopper question, but in fact it is the easiest one to answer. Thieves, murderers, and adulterers commit their crimes irrespective of whether they are religious or not. Once again, let me repeat: evil stems from the nature of man—nothing to do with religion. Though religious belief acts to suppress these evil inclinations of man's nature, man's own reasoning and inherent capability for good is even more effective as a restraint. If it were true that religion curbs criminal behavior, we would expect to find less crime in the more religiously active countries. In fact the opposite could be claimed. Using stats such as the number of homicides per capita, number of jailed prisoners per capita, number of teenage pregnancies, etc., the countries that have the lowest figures are clearly those with a higher percentage believing in evolution—a higher percent doubting the existence of God. The top countries are Japan, Norway, Britain, Germany, and Holland. Toward the bottom, we find America, where over 50 percent believe in God and only 40 percent in evolution and where homicide rates are five times those in Europe and ten times those in Japan. Though crime rates have dropped in America, it still ranked among the most violent of the industrialized nations, and I believe there is little doubt that it is among the most religious. While this may show that religion is not inversely proportional to crime, I would hesitate to support the corollary—that religion is proportional to crime. It could show, however, that violent crime is proportional to the availability of guns and that religion does nothing to stop it! The statistics just do not support the contention that atheist societies are more crime-ridden than religious ones.

In an atheist society, adultery will not be viewed as a sin against God but as a deviation from the accepted value and role of the monogamous married family in human society. The punishment hopefully will not be, in the absence of religion and the presence of reason, stoning to death, but the right to counseling and, ultimately, divorce. Murder will also not be a sin against God but an intolerable act against man's fundamental laws to be punished with all the severity it deserves. Punishment will not merely be based on retribution and reciprocity as in an eye for an eye, but will mirror the society's belief and ability to reform and treat offenders. In some instances, recognition will be given to causes other than "evil intent" like biological malfunctions, psychiatric illness, etc. In this context, sexual offenders may have a biological problem treatable by biological or chemical means. The point is there are no doctrinal constraints or restrictions as to how we evaluate and treat these crimes. We are free to evolve here as anywhere else as our knowledge and science advance. Humanism is very much a part of a world without God—an atheist world. As society and reason evolve, the inclination for crime will decrease. This is already evident in some of the more liberal (godless?) democratic societies. There will inevitably always be a distribution of the population that will remain criminal no matter whether the society is atheist or not. The atheist society will just be better prepared to work with this in the long run than the religious one.

The most difficult and taxing situation in deconstruction is the concept of afterlife or the immortal soul. This is the one belief that man created for himself that will be extremely difficult to eradicate. Weaning ourselves from the belief that the earth was (a) flat and (b) the center of the universe was a piece of cake compared to this one. At times I suspect that it was for this reason, the promise of eternal life, that we created the whole apparatus of a personal God and religion, or at least persisted in and perfected it. It is feared that without the incentives provided by afterlife theology, man will become self-serving and seek self-aggrandizement first and foremost. It is fear, plain and simple, of the end of life that has driven religion. Maybe we cannot do without religion after all! It is not surprising that of those atheists who have a change of heart and turn to God, it comes mostly in the latter stages of life: when the end draws near, death looms large, fear takes hold, and superstition is the remedial opiate.

While the belief in afterlife is thought to provide a strong incentive for moral behavior in this life, the opposite is actually the case. The belief in afterlife has assigned some of the responsibility for managing crime and punishment to God rather than man. As I stated earlier, morality is not a God-given set of values but is entirely man-made. Man, in such wisdom as he has developed to date, is perfectly aware that for his own good he should live his life by accepted moral principles. He is also aware that there will be digressions. For this purpose, there is law and order to discourage transgressions and take corrective action where they occur.

In the atheist world, law and order will take on a whole new meaning as it will be the last resort. There will be no final day of judgment. There will be a stronger incentive to provide the right environment to ensure greater compliance, more emphasis on inculcating moral value, and more rationalization. As I stated earlier, more attention could be paid to correction rather than retribution for wrongdoing. Rather than bringing religion to the impoverished and unemployed slums as a means to help them cope with their sad lot and thus gain entrance to heaven in the afterlife, efforts will be made to bring them out of poverty and to educate and employ them. With afterlife out of the equation altogether, the many "lucky" members of society will more clearly perceive that it is in their own clear interest to see that the few "unlucky" ones are given all possible options to get out of the ghetto, and the unlucky ones will see that it is to their advantage to take the opportunities offered and not turn to depravity. As we saw earlier, while religion did not cause most of the atrocities witnessed in the last century, it certainly did not stop them. If, leading up to that point, the world had, instead of religion, centuries of exposure to secular philosophy, would the outcomes have been as dire? Don't get me wrong. I do not believe that confrontations will not occur in a godless world. They will. Tragedies and even holocausts may yet be in our future. I just think we have a much better chance of avoiding them or minimizing them if all parties are informed by reason alone.

To get back to deconstructing God, it will not, indeed should not, be an abrupt, sudden event but a gradual process that started in ancient times and never really stopped. In ancient Greece, around the fifth century BC, Protagoras proposed that "man is the measure of all things" and questioned the existence of the gods. Socrates and the many other Greek philosophers established what later became scientific inquiry to move society away from myth to reality. Some two centuries earlier, the Charvaka philosophy in India, also known as the Lokayata, held that there is no such thing as the soul or afterlife or the gods, that existing religious scripts were the result of ignorance, and religious practices were for the convenience of the priests. All through history, I believe, you will always find people who questioned the established religion even when it was dangerous to do so. By definition, man was atheist before he created God. It is not surprising, therefore, that the seeds of atheism were sown in our ancient past, and religion, because it is false, never did kill the seed. The fact that atheism is only now flourishing is, I believe, because the soil is more fertile and the climate more favorable. Atheism today is not so much a studied intellectual reaction to a prevailing unchallenged hypothesis accepted and enforced by the majority, but the natural and logical conclusion that grows out of the vast and ever increasing evidence that our knowledge of the world provides. Science is the soil and freedom the climate. With this as the environment, reason blossoms and religion withers away.

Deconstruction could be said to have received a push forward back in the days of the French Revolution when an effort was made to make France an atheist state. Though it failed, and rightly so (it would have violated separation of church from state), it made atheism very much a part of the discourse, and today, France is closer to a-religiousness, humanism, and atheism than any other country in Europe. But as economists like to tell us when getting out of a particularly bad recession, it could get worse before it gets better. Take the recent spate of religiousness with its increasing introversion into human affairs—evident in American foreign policy, particularly during recent Republican presidencies and in Islamic states applying Sharia law to the dismay of an emancipated world. Take also the hijacking of Islam by extremists bent on wreaking havoc in non-Muslim and Muslim countries alike and in the process dishonoring everything Islam stands for. It is clear that deconstruction should somehow be accelerated and not left to the slow snail's pace and whims of our natural cultural evolution.

Let's talk some more about how to accelerate this process. First, I believe we should address how we should not proceed. I do not see any merit in ridiculing religion in an insulting, derogatory manner. The hate radio talk shows in the United States (I am sure this is also the case in other countries) only manage to inflame and incite one group against another, seeking sensationalism over justice. Yes, justice. We judge and find guilty with no semblance of a fair trial. To brand all of Islam as evil is itself an act of terrorism. The definition of terrorism is indiscriminate and vicious violence against the general population. Branding all of Islam as evil is indiscriminate, vicious, and clearly directed at all believers. Equally disturbing is the hurling of insults and disparaging treatment given to Muslims. The printing of the cartoons of Muhammad is an example. I know we cherish our freedom of expression and rightly so. I know that this is not a big deal to us, and we understand caricature for what it is. But surely, freedom entails responsibility. We should realize that such depictions are particularly sacrilegious to Muslims and would alienate the very people we need on our side—the vast majority of Muslims who are not terrorists.

OK, so Muslims are too sensitive. Maybe. But this is precisely the point. Which brings me back to how do we speed up deconstruction. We should encourage the conditions that result in people discovering for themselves what *we* have learned, and this will happen when they have the right mix of knowledge and freedom. As far as the world goes, Bush was not far off when he espoused the doctrine of bringing democracy to the Muslim world. However, this is easier said than done. We cannot impose democracy by force. We cannot impose democracy by supporting corrupt regimes. What we must be is determined, patient, and confident. Again, as stated earlier, we can invoke a Marshall Plan sense of urgency for the Middle East problem by being intensely but constructively involved. Also, we cannot impose democracy while not practicing it ourselves. The Muslim world sees no democracy in the creation of Israel. We certainly cannot impose separation of church and state abroad when our foreign policy often has or had a clear religious (albeit, we would like to think, not obvious) bias, and finally, we cannot impose morality without having staked out the high ground first. This goes back to what I said earlier in this chapter: it would help if we openly recognize our problems, past and present, and put our house in order before attempting to clean house for others. In this regard, President Obama took some significant steps with his speech in Cairo, June 2009, when he came as close as he could to saying that the war in Iraq was not exactly America's shining moment. His words: "I also believe that events in Iraq have reminded America of the need to use diplomacy and build international consensus to resolve our problems whenever possible." He deserves credit for sticking to this policy.

While we encourage all these virtues, it helps if we admit we are not perfect ourselves. To the hawks among us this is anathema. They are just plain wrong. No one is saying we renounce our military power. On the contrary, we make it absolutely clear that while we are a force for peace, we will not hesitate to strike at enemies who harm or threaten us or our allies. Initially, this policy will run into difficulties, but these will be far less than those we will otherwise encounter. What we must also do, and never stop, is educate and expose the target country or society to "modernity" using whatever legitimate means are at our disposal. We will fail in Afghanistan as long as the majority of the people are illiterate and uninformed and as long as half the population—women—are marginalized and disenfranchised. And we know how difficult it is to promote education against strongly held local traditions. Look at the controversy surrounding the teaching of evolution in our country!

I cannot overstress the importance of putting our house in order first. If we do not thoroughly eliminate religious influence from our politics and replace it with secular reasoning and give and take, we will find it very difficult to have a consistent, meaningful, and constructive foreign policy. Every presidential, indeed congressional, election will bring with it a threat of sweeping in a large group of Christian radicals. Our foreign policy will suddenly have religious undertones and deconstruction will fall back a heap.

The only genuinely moral ground is reached by renouncing all religious bias in politics and espousing reason as our compass—along the way both asserting our determination to have reason prevail on the world stage and recognizing that we have not been perfect. We can do no more. The rest is up to others. My hope is that this same spirit will eventually prevail the world over. I repeat here what I have said before. It is in our interest that democracy and economic and cultural prosperity spread across the world and that this happens as fast as possible. If, in the process, there is some leveling of prosperity—the prosperity of some will be reduced *in relation to others*—so be it. Perhaps it cannot be otherwise. In the future, it will become clear that each country cannot always have an increasing share of limited resources in relation to all others. At some point, those with the largest share will decrease relatively while others with the lowest increase. In some cases, the decrease might have to be absolute. The cake will not just be shared among more people—there will actually be a smaller cake. Resources are finite, and as their consumption grows, limitations will arise and accommodations will have to be made. If there will ever be a time for Reason to prevail, this will be it.

For sure there will be a full plate of problems the world will face that will spell disaster unless tackled by a secular approach worldwide. Energy, water, global warming, food, and biodiversity—to mention just a few of the resource-centered problems together with relations between the major regions of the world: the Americas, the Greater Middle East, Europe, Eurasia, Africa, and the Asia-Pacific regions. Believe me, while the will to solve these problems will have to be greater, so will the difficulty. In these circumstances, the last thing we need to bring to the table is the emotional and irrational mind-set that our religious beliefs demand. It would help at that point if our moral principles were based not on religious sentiment and doctrine but on reason and/or on principles with a great likelihood to be shared by all. Hopefully, technology might advance to the point where we may be able to synthesize materials as they become scarce, thereby ensuring enough for all. But until this happens, morality and reason will have to inform the sharing of resources. Incidentally, even when it comes to planet-related problems, there is no shortage of religious backing for unbridled despoiling based on God giving man full sway over the earth!

To summarize, let me state that the deconstruction of God is a gradual process. It started a long time ago but desperately needs to be sped up. The first, immediate goal must be to completely separate church and state—the world over, yes, but first, immediately, in our own country. (I was recently appalled by Senator Santorum's criticism of President Kennedy's adherence to "absolute" separation between church and state. What does separation mean, for Pete's sake? Is there any other kind of separation?) The goal must be to grill our politicians and ensure that they are not there to impose their religious beliefs, but have sound, reasoned bases for their policies. It is not a matter of questioning the faith they profess, but the extent to which a particular policy outcome is determined solely by a specific religious belief or even the extent to which their rationalizations will be subjected to and nuanced by their faith. This will hopefully remove religious overtones from our domestic and foreign policy and put it on a solid secular basis. A second immediate goal would be to make it abundantly clear that the highest morality is actually in the province of reason and not religion. The secular factions in our public life should take second row to no one—pope or pastor, Evangelicals or born-again. When religious leaders claim moral superiority, the secular establishment must immediately and publicly challenge them. We do not need to be lead and instructed, *we* need to step forward and be the moral leaders. A third goal would be to promote these same tendencies to the rest of the world. We may find, to our surprise, that parts of it are ahead of us and have been waiting for us to lead. We will also realize that it was just as well we changed because by that time, the whole world will have changed enormously—socially, politically, and economically. Finally, we are not talking about banning religion. Hopefully this will never happen, but with the natural evolution away from religion and toward reason, aided by an ever more relentless onslaught from the secular faction, I am confident that religion and belief in God will, by the end of this century, be of relatively minor significance in human affairs and, who knows, may eventually be totally eclipsed—like belief in a flat universe with the earth at its center.

Let me close this chapter with an exhortation I have already made. For deconstruction to flourish, we need not only a completely free society but a fully participative one. This is particularly the case during ELECTIONS. In those countries that *are* democracies and apropos of small minorities hijacking religions, why not make sure that *every* vote is cast, and that every person who is old enough to vote does vote? Where the majority are apathetic and do not vote, it is much too easy for a minority backed with huge sums of money to hijack an election by mobilizing enough votes. Personally, I love the idea of making voting obligatory. I believe Argentina has a system close to this and Australia an even more successful one. It is my dream, also, that voting takes place over a weekend, say, Saturday and Sunday and, say, in September, making it much more accessible to voters in terms of work, school, weather, and religious observance (yes, atheists can, after all, be accommodating to all belief systems). Not on a cold Tuesday in November. Besides all the tremendous advantages that would result, the one that concerns me here is that deconstruction would occur at a much faster pace when everybody participates. If it does not, so be it. The right conditions will arise soon enough. Alas, I fear that this is wishful thinking (electoral reform)—achieving it is about as likely as achieving absolutely impartial and logical (geographically speaking) voting districts.

End Notes

(6.1) Fix reason firmly in her seat, and call to her tribunal every, http://www.brainyquote.com/quotes/quotes/t/thomasjeff141347.html (accessed September 13, 2015).

(6.2) Religious views of Thomas Jefferson—Wikipedia, the free, http://en.wikipedia.org/wiki/Thomas_Jefferson_and_religion (accessed September 13, 2015).

(6.3) Pat Robertson: Haiti 'Cursed' By 'Pact To The Devil' (VIDEO), http://www.huffingtonpost.com/2010/01/13/pat-robertson-haiti-curse_n_422099.html (accessed September 13, 2015).

(6.4) Pat Robertson Lays The Blame For The 2001 World Trade Center Terrorist Attacks. http://www.snopes.com/rumors/falwell.asp (accessed September 21, 2015)

CHAPTER 7

THE LAST WORD

> To put the world in order, we must first put the nation in order; to put the nation in order, we must first put the family in order; to put the family in order; we must first cultivate our personal life; we must first set our hearts right.
>
> —Confucius

The first volume of the great British statesman Winston Churchill's *The Second World War* was titled *The Gathering Storm,* where he wrote eloquently of the many signs of potential disaster that emanated from Germany during the '20s and '30s and were completely, often blithely, ignored. I sometimes wonder if today we are witnessing a series of events occurring around us that if ignored and not managed appropriately, could lead to even more dire consequences, and I ask myself if much like the generation before World War II, we are just as blithely going about our business as usual, incapable or unwilling to deal with it. Are we failing to recognize the writing on the wall?

Essential to this scenario is the realization that we are at a stage where our physical evolution continues at a snail's pace and with it the evolution of the part of our brain that is hardwired, but apace with this is the evolution of our soft-wired selves that is accelerating beyond our ability to manage it. Our knowledge, creativity, and innovation have picked up enough speed to launch us into a world as unreal as any our forebears could ever have imagined. As far as they are concerned, we might as well be an alien species on another planet. Why, we can even clone ourselves and have certainly made virgin birth commonplace! We are even poised to take over the physical evolution of our species, radically changing our genetic makeup. Fortunately, I do not see the latter happening in my or even my grandchildren's lifetime, but who knows. Throw into this mix our ability to manipulate the environment to a point that may indeed result in an alien planet and threaten our very existence, and you have a recipe for disaster. Unless we harness our potential, manage our progress, and control the process, we are in for an extremely bumpy ride—the gathering storm could prove disastrous and find us woefully unprepared just as it did in the last century.

In the widening chasm between our hardwired and soft-wired selves, we have religion. Religion has tried to catch up and adapt to the new paradigm, but even the more liberal denominations fall far short, and some, particularly Islam, are way too inflexible to allow for anything other than outright confrontation. Like tectonic plates pushing up against each other, something will eventually give, and when this happens—look out world! In a time when we need a well-oiled piece of machinery to steer us through our difficulties, religion throws sand in the gears and makes life hell.

It is my contention, as I explained earlier, that the only way out of this dilemma is for religion to bow out or be nudged out of the picture altogether. It will not be the first time in our history when a shift of such magnitude has occurred. Shamans and medicine men bowed out as the science of medicine emerged to take their places. Witchcraft and oracles withdrew against the onslaught of reason. OK, there are still some nuts around who "dabble" here and there—exceptions who prove the rule. If the more cohesive philosophies of today's major religions did not force paganism to wither away, surely it would have, anyway, before the onslaught of science showing the sun and the moon to be mere objects of gas, rocks, and star dust. It is time we recognize that our religions today are equally out of place as other institutions before them. Take monarchies, for instance. Their time came and went. The ones that survive have had to adapt big time and bear little resemblance to their former selves. Historians like to speculate that ultimately, democracy and capitalism in some form will spread across the whole world and refer to that period as the end of history, since not much will change after that and history is all about change. Personally, I have my doubts for, as we speak, man is "fixing", as they say south of the Dixie line, to change his very species, and that will give us change a while longer.

At the risk of repeating myself, however, the only adaptation available to religion is to cease existing in its current state! To cease binding man's psyche to a past that was delusional at best, and to allow it to flourish in today's reality. In today's world, and certainly in the future, we cannot have people at the head of powerful, history-making nations use their interpretations of scripture and the prophesies therein as justification for war or as justification for policies that do little to prevent and, in fact, hasten the gathering storm. George W. Bush is reported to have referred to certain biblical references when he sought support for the proposed invasion of Iraq from Jacques Chirac, the president of France. It would be pointless to relate the outrageous quotes by some of the Islamist political and religious leaders praising suicide bombers, denying the Holocaust, calling for the extermination of Israel, and predicting that Islam will one day rule the world (utterly convinced, it would seem, that Allah is on their side). And there's Hindu extremism in India, Buddhist extremists in Sri Lanka, religious extremists in Israel, and on and on. There is no doubt that there is enough religious extremism and division in the world to keep the pot boiling for generations to come; and when the pot boils, there is always the danger that it will boil over or blow the lid off and create a god-almighty mess, as has all too often been the case in the past.

I do not want to rehash the preceding chapter. I cannot conclude this short book, however, without a final call to REASON. There are too many challenges facing our species to not pool our resources and move forward together, more or less in the same direction. Opportunities, not challenges, may be a better way to view them.

One such challenge or opportunity is the Arab Spring. Here is a movement that cries out for wise management. On December 17, 2010, in a small town of Sidi Bouzid, Tunisia, a simple twenty-six-year-old man, Mohamed Bouazizi, as was his way, had set up his street-side cart to sell produce, so he could eke out a living for himself, his mother and siblings. He had become a fixture in the place, much loved by some, tolerated by others, and appreciated by all who knew him and bought his wares. Around 10 a.m. that fateful morning, not unlike many occasions before, he was once again harassed by one of the local officials who seemed to believe their job was to make life unbearable for people such as Bouazizi. They would demand permits that were highly questionable, confiscate his goods, accept bribes, and generally screw with him, to put it mildly. This was quite commonplace in Tunisia, as I suspect it was, and is, across many parts of the Arab world—a vast region dominated by Islam and composed of mostly authoritarian states whose peoples were long exposed to the harsh realities of life and to the harsh bureaucracies that intruded in their lives, with no right whatsoever, and took pleasure in destroying their destinies. This morning, Bouazizi was publicly humiliated and his cart wheeled off without further ado. Many confrontations with authority ended that way, with a peremptory confiscation, in this case, of property. It was too much for him, the last straw, enough was enough. After unsuccessfully trying to be heard at the governor's office, he went off, got a can of gasoline, came back and doused himself with it and set himself on fire to protest the injustice and the indignities suffered by himself and, it turned out, by his fellow citizens. Bouazizi died eighteen days later, on January 4, 2011, after attempts to save him failed. Little did this wretched man realize that his horrific immolation would be the spark that ignited an already smoldering population. Almost immediately, outrage gave way to public protests, and the unrest grew to such alarming proportions, despite efforts to subdue it, that President Ben Ali fled the country on January 14, 2011, just ten days later!

Almost overnight, or so it seemed, a wave, no, a tsunami of protests swept over the whole region—spanning all of North Africa to parts of the Middle East. Not a single country there was spared. Governments fell, as well, in Egypt, Libya, and Yemen. The protests were subdued in Algeria with the lifting of the nineteen-year-old state of emergency and in Sudan after President Bashir announced he would not seek reelection. He had been president since 1993, for heaven's sake, some eighteen years! In most of the other states, political and/or economic concessions were obtained. One of the states where turmoil is still ongoing and has degenerated into a shocking display of state-sanctioned violence is Syria, a state with one of *the* most authoritarian governments. Unsurprisingly, after a year of strife, Syria has become a country on the verge of civil war with massive repression and carnage.

I wrote the above four years ago! At that time I also wrote: Will the world step up to the plate and intervene? Does it know how this should be done? Even if it did, would Russia and China cooperate? Here we have a situation fraught with danger, yes, but with potential too. In this vast region, change is afoot and it is up to us to steer it in the right direction—not our direction, necessarily, but the right direction. Religion will continue to play a huge role in the region. It is so entrenched here that it will not recede to insignificance overnight. But the Arabs must make a choice: Will they emerge as a freer but still radically closed Islamist society? Will they emerge as a thoroughly modern democratic society, or at the very least, if it has to be religious, will there emerge a new golden age of Islam, much like the progressive, open, inclusive Islamist society of yore? Will reason temper religion, or will religious and sectarian hatred prevail?

What do I know! What a difference four years can make. The situation in Syria has become so horrific that I will treat it in an epilogue. But Syria aside, practically all the Arab countries involved in the Arab Spring have had their initial gains rolled back and have reverted to situations of little to no freedom. One exception is Tunisia itself, where they have recently celebrated free elections and are well on their way to join the ranks of the "emancipated." If only Mohamed Bouazizi had lived to see the change he wrought!

Though the overall outcome of the Arab Spring has been disappointing, let Tunisia serve as the silver lining in the dark clouds amassed over the Middle East. It is naive to suggest that religion can be vanquished or self-destruct overnight in the Middle East. It will take a long time and require our commitment to the long haul. The Arab Spring was just the beginning—the first quake in what could be a series of quakes before the big one hits. Things could get a lot worse before they get better. Consider the emergence of ISIL.

Well aware of his dark side, man is just as aware of his sublime potential. Man is given to dreams and wonder that serve to enhance and inspire his reason. It is this side that must now be summoned to provide the impetus going forward. Religion clearly helped in the past, though not always. Today it is more of a hindrance and clearly obsolete or in need of significant adaptation. Today, with an intact set of morals and values, man is poised for the great leap forward. Religion will merely tend to impede his progress. This should not be allowed to happen!

Reason buttressed by dreams has triumphed over religion in the past and there is no reason it cannot do so again. The manner in which this has happened may not have been too obvious because it appeared with some religious undertones. Let me give you a few of my favorite examples.

Some 2,300 years ago, in the third century BC, there was a man who was a king, whose kingdom, through a series of bloody conquests, extended over most of the Indian subcontinent. His name was Ashoka. One of his last epic conquests had resulted in so much bloodshed and slaughter of innocent victims that it shook him to the core, and he vowed to change. Like many before him, and since, he had a transformational moment. He reasoned and dreamed, dreamed and reasoned, and lived out the rest of his life searching for a better way. His empire became a land where nonviolence was policy and all citizens were equal, where even the common man had access to universities. The king was not of divine origin but required the approval of the Buddhist *sangha* (which in those early days could have meant an assembly of elders or monks). Health care was provided, where possible, for both the human and animal populations, with treatment facilities and availability of medicinal herbs. Environmental protection was instituted by laws restricting animal slaughter, cruelty, and the burning or indiscriminate cutting down of trees and forests. Vegetarianism was encouraged and infrastructure was put in place by digging wells and ensuring adequate water supply.

In all probability, such enlightenment did not permeate every corner of the land nor affect every citizen, and it certainly did not last. But it was clearly attempted, and this alone is a stunning testament to man. Ashoka claimed no divine inspiration, intervention, or dialogue—just a man's sickening with the evil around him and a firm resolution to create a better world. In a sense, though, it has survived. As his most lasting legacy, Ashoka did for Buddhism what Emperor Constantine did for Christianity some 570 years later. He embraced this least theocratic and most peaceful of all religions and exported it to the far corners of the earth, certainly all across India and into Sri Lanka, where his son, Mahindra, and daughter, Sanghamitra, were sent as proselytizers. India's flag today carries Ashoka's *chakra* (wheel) in the center, symbolizing *dharma* (or universal law). India's national emblem is an image of the lion sculpture atop the Ashoka pillar at Sarnath, featuring four lions standing back-to-back.

I mention this not only because it is one of my favorite stories from the past but because it is one of the most inspirational and one of the most credible. Bear in mind that little, if any, archaeological or other hard evidence has been found for any of *our* biblical figures. Most of their stories were written centuries after the fact as was Ashoka's too. But in Ashoka's case, the stories are backed up by hard contemporaneous evidence that exists in the solid limestone pillars he had erected across his kingdom bearing an account of who he was and the good news of his reign. Ashoka showed that no matter how far one falls there is no limit to how high one could soar. In my opinion, it is not coincidental that Ashoka embraced Buddhism, which, we have already seen, is by far the religion least concerned with God. Some even say it is an atheist religion. Ashoka was able to rise up not so much because a God personally intervened in his life, but because of a personal encounter with his own conscience—a testament to the strength of human compassion and human will to overcome human limitations. Ashoka showed that hell is of *our* own making, and if there is to be a paradise here on earth, that it should be created by us mere mortals who could yet be gods.

Some two hundred and fifty years before Ashoka, in the year 551 BC, a man was born not to be a king, but as the son of the concubine of a famous warrior. Or so goes one of the legends surrounding his life, because unlike Ashoka, no contemporaneous etched-in-stone records were found, and we only have accounts written centuries after he lived. Be that as it may, the story goes that when he was three, his father died, and Confucius and his mother lived in poverty until her death when he was seventeen. At twenty he married, but despite marital and familial contentment, his restlessness got the better of him, and he set off to pursue his dreams and to follow his own reason. Confucius had studied as much as he could all his life and learning had become an obsession with him. His dream was to define, improve, and then redefine the civilization he was born into. How fortunate for the world that this man lived when he did and showed the world that one's destiny lies in one's own hands. How fortunate that he did not wait around for God to intervene and establish a new religion but went about the straightforward task that he himself had chosen, making it his life's work. His precepts were clear—it is not about doctrine and dogma, it's about promoting the highest moral and ethical standards by example and study. You teach by example and behavior, and you keep an open mind and never assume you have all the answers. He believed that man should constantly strive to learn more about himself and the world around him, while faithfully following a precise moral compass. Morality and ethics the world over owe a great debt to this man. Confucius left his mark not only on the civilization of his time but all through the ages, and not only in his part of the world, the Far East, but all across the globe. It is believed by some that through translations of his work into Latin in the mid-seventeenth century, he even influenced the thinkers of the European Enlightenment. It is no wonder that he has been one of the most quoted of all time.

As far as I know, none of the Greek philosophers claimed divine inspiration for their accomplishments even if they went along with the attributes of some of the contemporary deities. The point I am making here is that humanity can do quite well without religion, thank you! History is full of magnificent examples of man reaching for and achieving true greatness without divine intervention. In ethics, morality, science, the arts, philosophy, and politics, it has become abundantly clear that our future is ours to steer, not God's or the Devil's, and man can continue advancing in all these areas without religion muddying the waters. I am not saying that religion cannot help. I am saying that it can also most definitely hurt, and who's to play referee, controlling such a behemoth? Better to continue into the future without it, wouldn't you agree? Here is a truth so self-evident that it should require no apology whatsoever: *everything man is today, good or bad, is due entirely to his physical and intellectual capacity* (a corollary of this is that everything we ascribe to God as we know him has first originated in our intellect since we created God). If we accept this, we will no longer need religion. If we do not accept this, then we must continue on our journey a while longer dealing with excess baggage and obstacles along the way, all of our own creation! Which will it be?

The Bible begins with the words, "In the beginning," and the last word is "Amen." I hope that this book dispels the fanciful accounts of creation provided by the major religions and places it in a robust, modern, rational context. As for the last word, I will be hard put to say amen, because, whereas a religious text can presume to have said it all and end further discussion with a conclusive amen, I am only reminded that though we have come a long way in our understanding of our history, there is still so much to learn. We feel fairly certain about the knowledge we have acquired and confident about discarding the beliefs we were spoon fed over the centuries, but the more we learn, the more there is out there, taunting and humbling us. In a way this is good as it gives us more to look forward to.

It is indeed humbling to admit that some of the questions we started out with in the first chapters have still not been answered, even remotely! Why are we here, what is the purpose of it all? Answering the how, when, and where questions are one thing, but answering the why question is quite another. Now we are talking philosophical questions that religion supposedly provided the answers for, answers we now know were figments of our own imagination. Philosophers have wrestled with this problem from time immemorial. Unfortunately, I find some of the philosophers' answers even more fanciful. The truth, when it arrives, may be far simpler than anything imagined to date, and probably obvious too. But feel free to explore the trends in philosophy on this subject, and good luck to you. I, for one, find the language philosophers use too surreal and confusing, and I believe this muddies the water even more. It reminds me of the aversion I have to legalese, the language lawyers use. Why, for heaven's sake, do we insist on writing our laws in archaic terms using the words and constructions of Latin, a great language in its day, but one that has been dead for close to two thousand years? When will we start to use simple modern English or Spanish, whatever? OK, OK, I am glad that Latin and Greek were around and contributed as much as they have to the structure and richness of so many modern languages, and make no mistake, the contribution is enormous, but that said, can we please use simple contemporary prose to frame our laws?

I understand that the concepts being developed by philosophers are extremely abstract and ordinary language may not quite be up to the task, but on the other hand, I feel not enough effort is being made to keep it simple. It is almost as if the more fanciful the terms used, the greater the aura of legitimacy imparted to the thesis. To me, philosophical discussions sometimes resemble abstract modern art. For instance, I can appreciate the drama of Picasso's *Guernica,* but I fail to see the art in, say, a Jackson Pollock painting. But what do I know!

One of the reasons science has advanced so much in the last centuries, I believe, is that language, and our own English language is a good example of that, has evolved apace. There is increasing evidence that language determines, to some extent, how we think. A recent article in *Scientific American* (was it in 2011?) addresses this point and gives many examples. One impressive example was the case of the Australian aborigines who, when asked to close their eyes and point in a certain direction of the compass, had no difficulty doing so, no matter the direction they were asked to point to. On the other hand, when audiences in Stanford, Harvard, and Oxford Universities were asked to close their eyes and do the same, the results were shockingly disappointing! It turns out that in the language of the aborigines, directions are described only in terms of geographic directions. You placed your fork on the west of the plate and the knife on the east (if you were facing north, I suppose), and so on. Your language incorporated and became an extension of your innate orientation skill.

We may have to wait for *language* to evolve further just as knowledge of our brain, and indeed, mind, evolves before we can satisfactorily address some of these issues. So if the question is why are we here, I am unable to provide an answer, particularly if you are looking for a rational explanation. Do we have a special purpose in the overall scheme of things? No, I do not currently think so. I mean, after all, it looks like we are here both as a result of a controlled process (natural selection) and random events (planetary conditions). I do not see a purpose in that, especially as it relates to us as a species. We have potential, yes, but *purpose?* We have the potential to save or destroy this planet, for instance! Again, just saying!

If the question is why did the universe come into existence in the first place, if indeed its existence is not directly and very presumptuously dependent on ours, I do not have the answer to that either. Does this mean I must abdicate my search for a rational, natural answer and search instead for the supernatural? No! It just means that at this point in time we do not know. Live with it! At the beginning of this chapter, I stated that there is so much to be learned. The absence of knowledge should not frighten us or force us to seek solace in superstitious belief. It merely means we should patiently pursue rational investigation and, in the process, live like the rational beings we are.

In fact, we may never have answers to all our questions. Scientists are beginning to wonder if the physical limitations of our brain will at some point put a cap on our ability to increase our knowledge any further. For example, the distance traveled by brain pulses and the resulting time taken may prove to be a cap on the complexity of the thought processes. Increasing the number of brain cells or the physical size of the brain is not much of an option: the brain is already at optimal size given (a) the (maximum) size of the birth canal as explained in a previous chapter; and (b) if the size *were* to increase, the distance/cycle time factor would worsen considerably and so on. By working in groups, in stages, and using computers, we can extend the cap, so to speak, but there is doubt as to whether we can eventually know all there is to know.

Be that as it may, we should capitalize on what we do know. We know that we exist (come on, let's not get philosophical here), that we have much intelligence, that we have free will, and that we can dream. We know that we are also instinctive and gregarious creatures whose survival depends on social cohesion. We know this gives us tremendous power over our lives and even the planet. We can define and distinguish between good and evil. We can identify and control what gives quality to our lives. We can even effect changes in our own species, and of course, we can always succumb to ignorance. Armed with this knowledge, it only remains for us to survive and continue to evolve while pursuing as much happiness, progress, and fulfillment as we can in our lives, both at the individual and social levels. Even if we have not fathomed the initial why, we should ask ourselves if we can define and affirm a meaningful purpose going forward. Our existence could take on a whole new significance—one that we will impart and manage. That, for now, is not only why we are here but how lucky we are to be here. That is good news for me. I hope it is GOOD NEWS FOR YOU too. And with that, I hope we can all say, until further enlightenment comes our way, *amen.*

EPILOGUE

In the prologue of this book, I mentioned that I set myself the goal to write it as a New Year's resolution on Dec. 31, 1999, the infamous Y2K date. Actually, I started to research it shortly thereafter, but it wasn't until 2006 that I finally sat down and started putting it all together, finishing it by 2008. All I wanted, I thought, was for my grandchildren to read this at some point and get a feel for who I really was and what I felt was important. I was reluctant to publish the book. However, I found myself going back to it time and time again, to check punctuation or a turn of phrase and, inevitably, to update to current affairs which, if I remember correctly, was after the Arab Spring in 2011. So here I am now in February 2015 getting updated once more and for the last time. How time flies! On rereading my book, I feel it has stood the test of time fairly well—but I may be biased.

During this four-year period, a lot of water has gone under the bridge, and I cannot resist giving my take on at least one major change in the political landscape. Know what I am talking about? What else but the Middle East. I am referring, of course, to ISIS or ISIL or whatever it is they go by.

When George Bush invaded Iraq, little did he think it would help spawn such evil. But like all Monday morning quarterbacks, it's really easy to see that all the conditions were already there. Religious fanatics exist in all religions, and over the years, fodder had been provided to maintain and even grow them till they reached critical mass. It can't all be laid at George Bush's feet!

First, from the West's maneuvers to safeguard oil supplies for well over the last hundred years, we allied ourselves with and supported authoritarian, unpopular regimes like those in Iran, Saudi Arabia, Egypt, and so on. You name it. In every instance, the desires of the local populations were of no importance to the West.

Second, as victors in two major global wars, we carved up territories and established nations and their borders, again with little consideration for the local populations, resulting in synthesized states with illogical national boundaries and juxtaposition of ethnicities and religious sects bound to fester and lead to severe problems, especially with no constitutional protections for minorities.

Third, if the above did not suffice, by creating a brand-new state and filling it with people brought from Europe, of yet another religion long held in poor regard in the region, creating in the process what really amounts to an infranational territory with a humiliated, dispossessed people that serves as a constant cause of rage in the whole of the Arab world.

Never mind that we are only human and were protecting our own interests—it is still shameful. After suffering two world wars plus those in Korea and Vietnam, the West should have been fully aware of and sensitive to the conditions prevailing locally. We should have acted more intelligently and responsibly, not with a to-the-victor-go-the-spoils attitude but with a let's-get-this-right-for-the-future-of-everyone attitude, taking not just our own immediate needs and security into consideration.

Did we believe then, as too many still do, that Arabs are kind of second-class, and Muslims, in particular, are a violent lot anyway? Did we then, and do we still now believe they were and are a hopelessly fanatical, unruly, uncivilized lot? Or did our own governments succumb to minority power blocs with these bigoted views? I am not a politician or a statesman, so I can speak freely. I would just point out that Winston Churchill, one of my heroes, albeit with significant shortcomings, was notorious for his contempt of non-Aryan peoples. Ishaan Tharoor, foreign affairs writer for the *Washington Post* and a former senior editor of *Time* magazine, posted an article on February 3, 2015 that reported Churchill referring to Palestinians as "barbaric hordes who ate little but camel dung."

I believe the West then, and too many of us now, do not treat the Arabs and, in some cases, the Muslims, as equals. Here is why I say this. I do not believe we afford them the same dignity or esteem that we afford ourselves as a people. Either that, or we have been guilty of wanton ignorance. I mean why else would we create the state of Iraq with such disparate divisions of people, ethnic and otherwise: the Shia majority in the south, the Kurdish minority in the north, and the Sunni minority everywhere else and in charge of it all. A disaster waiting to happen. And why else would we be sensitive to these issues in our dealings with postwar Europe but insensitive when it came to the Middle East? OK, it could be argued that these borders are not so different than in the past, even under the Ottoman Empire. No matter. With sentiments such as Churchill's expressed so openly, there was absolutely no chance of in-depth, long-term, deep, and thoughtful consideration given to change things for the better going forward—for instance, insisting on certain constitutional safeguards for the various sects and minorities. Just saying, what do I know!

And let us be frank. A large portion of the blame must lie with the local Middle East populations themselves. Given that we in the West were remarkably remiss in our actions, why could the local people not finally take charge of their own destinies? When is Saudi Arabia going to modernize its society? The whole Arab world in fact? For how long does the rest of the world wait and world order be threatened while intrafaith strife ensues to see how much more retro each side could be instead of how progressive?

Let us also be aware that what we are really talking about is the future of the whole world. What happens on one side of the globe TODAY affects the whole globe. This is modern reality. Simply retreating from the world's imbroglios and letting others make their own beds to lie in is tantamount to ensuring disasters in the future. Do we really believe that it would be perfectly all right, for example, for half the world to have remained in the Dark Ages, never to emerge from them? Of course not! No one that I can think of denies that promoting modern knowledge, technology, and science across the globe is not only necessary but contributes mightily to global security and well-being.

Getting rid of cars and replacing them with horses and carriages is not an option to reverse global warming. We will have to come up, and will come up, with modern solutions. Where our science has shown us that previously held beliefs and practices were wrong or new practices are required, we change them. For example, we vaccinate and inoculate our infants to prevent the incidence and spread of disease, or we recognize that women are as smart as men and treat them as equals. Our mores change, our lives change. Change is an absolute, a given. It brought us here, and it will take us where we are going. Resistance to change dooms a society to failure and dysfunction.

Why is it so difficult, then, to accept that we must do everything in our power to ensure that the enlightened progress that we as a species are experiencing is not hindered or reversed by rejection of the new norms wherever that may be happening? If some societies were to legalize slavery, should the rest of the world accept that as a state's right and not seek to reverse it? If others were to allow human sacrifice, should we stand idly by? I hope not! If America's Supreme Court ruled that the second amendment allows an individual to "keep and bear" nuclear weapons if they were no larger than a briefcase, should they be allowed to do so? Or a handgun-sized, *Star Wars* gun that could cut a swathe through a multitude? Should the world stand idly by? Should we even sanction its manufacture?

In the August 2015 publication of *Scientific American,* there is an excellent article by Curtis W. Marean, professor at the School of Human Evolution and Social Change at Arizona State, that postulates this remarkable thesis: "Two innovations unique to H. sapiens primed our species for world domination: a genetically determined propensity for cooperation with unrelated individuals and advanced projectile weapons." A further interesting aspect of his thesis is that these factors came into play mainly in those situations where a group or groups of people had to protect and assure availability of much needed and densely occurring resources like food supply, water, etc. In terms of today, think oil, water, and so on and—a certain type of land! The land of Israel might be barren and unappealing geographically, but boy, is it extremely valuable and scarce from the ethnic/ religious point of view! And let us not forget—the whole planet is a "dense" resource. If rendered uninhabitable, it would be so for each and every one of us. What happens in one remote part could quickly spread to the whole world. Look at Ebola or the Arab Spring. And now look at ISIS.

It is a shame that we as a species are failing in the cooperative propensities and excelling in the projectile weaponry when faced with these issues. Are we failing and thwarting our own evolution, and where will this all lead? It is ironic that Obama, the first president to embrace cooperation, dialog, and negotiation, is the most maligned for these reasons! America has the projectiles but not the cooperative genes, Obama excluded.

Why then do we not react to grievous breaches of accepted norms perpetrated daily in the name of religion? Why do we not react to religion's stark persistence and refusal to adapt or cooperate in the face of irrefutable challenges to our well-being? It bears repeating. The whole planet is at risk when just a part is infected. We cannot accept that girls are not allowed access to learning. We cannot allow a couple to be stoned to death for adultery. We cannot allow even the church to blatantly disregard what have become patently accepted and required norms and expect no consequences.

Just recently, it was reported that the California Supreme Court struck down the law allowing parents to have their children exempted from immunization vaccines on religious grounds. About time, I say. It is time that accepted human rights codes trump any and all religious guidelines to the contrary. Certain issues trump religious dogma: public health and public safety are two of them.

Which brings me back to the Middle East and Islam. For a long time now, as the world adapts to modern influences and establishes norms for society, it is becoming apparent that there is a wide gap between these norms and the norms of orthodox Muslim societies. It is apparent that this gap is widening and becoming more striking with each passing day. We are aware of it, and they are aware of it. Bridging this gap becomes ever more problematical.

Moderates do exist in Muslim societies. But is what they understand as moderate something we would consider so? In June 2015 there was a heat wave in Pakistan. Temperatures rose to 112.64 °F on the second day and dipped slightly the next few days. There were one thousand deaths reported. One of the contributing factors to such a high toll is that this was happening in the middle of Ramadan and too many people stubbornly stuck to the fasting protocol—no food or drink from dawn to sunset. Now as an atheist, I cannot think of anything more anachronistic than that. Surely these people are not all extremists. Many of them or most must consider themselves to be mainstream. What does this tell us about the degree of difficulty to get them from where they are to accepting that such religious practices need to be discarded and new ones adopted more in line with modern knowledge, if you will?

It is in such societies—first in Iraq then in Syria, to name just two—that severe disorder and divisions were created largely by their own inability and lack of will to come to terms with their diversity, but also, and more immediately, by the rest of the world fanning the flames whether by ill-advised interventions (Iraq) or ill-conceived strategies with allies (not tough enough on Saudi Arabia or the Shia majority in Iraq or the Israel-Palestine situation, etc.) or lackluster support against terrorism from would-be world players like Russia and China.

ISIS arose like a phoenix out of the ashes of Al-Qaeda of Iraq which the Iraqis themselves had subdued with help from the Americans. After the Americans pulled out, however, old rivalries, distrust, and hatred surfaced once more (not that they had really gone away). The predominantly Shia government ruled supreme with token positions for Sunni and Kurdish members. Disillusion and detachment returned, this time to the Sunni minority, whose ranks were swelled by even more young, *idled* men when the Americans disbanded Saddam's army of mostly Sunni men, a minority enraged even further by constant snubs from the Shia majority and their close ties to the Shia of Iran. This is the VACUUM I was talking about within the Sunni population. Into this scenario, into this vacuum steps an individual: Abu Bakr Al-Baghdadi.

He had been jailed by the Americans in February 2004 and released in December as a "civilian detainee." It is said that he was "turned" during that period and quickly impressed and became a leader of the disenchanted Sunni captives in that prison. He quickly rose through the ranks of Al-Qaeda in Iraq, otherwise known as Islamic State of Iraq, and became its leader in May 2010. During the next two years, he oversaw several ISI attacks in Iraq. Persecution of Shia infidels has been a constant goal of his.

In 2013, he moved into Syria, joined with Jabhat al-Nusra, the Syrian extension of Al-Qaeda in Iraq, and announced the formation of Islamic State of Iraq and Levant (ISIL), also known as Islamic State of Iraq and Syria (ISIS). In June 2014, ISIS announced the establishment of a worldwide CALIPHATE with Al-Baghdadi as CALIPH. Our civilian detainee had come a long way since incarceration in February 2004!

The rest, as they say, is history. Take the most brutal interpretations of the KORAN, call it SHARIA law or whatever, and then raise this to a new level and you will have an idea of ISIS. It is widely accepted that their ultimate goal is to return to medieval concepts of Islamic law, Islamic society, and the Islamic State. Also to reject modern civilization and to bring on the APOCALYPSE. Recent estimates have them at between nine thousand to eighteen thousand strong, with the ability to grow to thirty thousand. Some six thousand fighters have been killed by coalition forces. It is also well known that thousands of young men and women the world over are wanting to participate in this so-called holy war either by traveling to the Middle East or acting alone or in small groups at home. Their tactics of brutal killings have spread to the West, and no country or city is safe. Gruesome videos of beheadings and the like are routinely posted on the Internet, both to spread terror and to recruit would-be terrorists. The irony of it all is that while they embrace modern technology to achieve their goals, their aim is to return to medieval, brutal times.

So much for the update! Before I leave you, dear readers, please allow me to summarize what we have learned on this journey and suggest actions so that all will not be lost when we return to our daily lives:

Summary

1. The personal God man adores simply does not exist. *We created Him and religion.* We know this from our science-based understanding of the origin of the universe and the origin of man.
2. We are fully aware that we, and only we, are the masters of our destiny, not some non-existent supernatural being or force.
3. Mankind is at an incredibly significant threshold today. He has immense knowledge and, therefore, immense power. Power that can be used for good or evil. His decision and his alone!
4. Morality is not the province of a particular religion or religion in general. Morality is part of man's nature. Atheists are just as moral, if not more so, than believers. By the same token, evil is not the province of atheists alone— all men, believers included, are subject to its snares.
5. This situation puts us on a collision course with religion and religious beliefs and there will be an inevitable struggle, violent if we lose control or non violent if managed well.

Global Action

1. Going forward ATHEISM WILL UNIVERSALLY BE CONSIDERED A SYSTEM OF BELIEF ON A PAR WITH OTHER RELIGIONS, WITH ALL THE ATTENDING RIGHTS, INCLUDING FREEDOM OF PROFESSION AND PRACTICE.
2. It must be agreed upon at a global level that no human being, no matter where in the world, can be persecuted for his beliefs, including ATHEISTS,. Every human being has the right to openly profess his or her creed, including ATHEISTS! This will apply to the United States and to Saudi Arabia, to India and to Pakistan, to every human being, everywhere!
3. National sovereignty will not include the right to prohibit an individual from professing his belief, and nations will be obliged to ensure that citizens uphold this right. Atheism is not blasphemy and will not result in punishment, or putting to death. In other words, no nation's sovereignty trumps the basic inalienable rights of its citizens to freely choose their beliefs, INCLUDING ATHEISM!
4. Article 18 of the United Nations Declaration of Human Rights should be amended to state explicitly that Atheism is clearly entitled to these same protections., and that Freedom of Worship includes the freedom to be an atheist. At the same time, blatant disrespect for others' beliefs will be discouraged — recent inflammatory caricatures of religious figures are a case in point. The advance in civilization referred to earlier calls for more respectful and, hopefully, more effective ways to disagree.
5. On December 10 each year, the United Nations celebrates Human Rights Day. It is suggested that on every fourth such celebration, coinciding with a Summer Olympics year, each member state shall publish this Declaration of Human Rights, so that each and every citizen will have access to it if desired.

For America.

1. As the leader of the free world and defender of democracy America must put its house in order, starting with the outdated electoral system. Gerrymandering must end. Obligatory and early voting must be put in place. We must deal with varying term durations and varying renewal calendars of our elected representatives, and make Congress, the Senate and the Presidency all subject to the same four year terms, and all renewable in the same year. We must alter the Senate's imbalance or disproportionality, where relatively more representation is given to the less populated states. We should form more political parties, put an end to the utterly inappropriate campaign finance laws, and generally resemble, even surpass the more enlightened nations out there or risk becoming the *military* or *entertainment* or *capitalist* leader of the Free World not simply "*the* leader".
2. Let us once again affirm our belief that the Constitution is a living instrument. Far better to amend than stretch it to absurd extremes that put our society in jeopardy and stagnation. Far better to perceive our country as we perceive our infrastructure, that, like all things human, it needs maintaining, it needs updating, it needs to reflect our relevance to our time and place in history. Remember, our Constitution, like God, was also made by man, it is really not infallible!
3. Atheists in this country should stand up and be counted. They should stake out the highest moral ground and concede nothing to the other factions in this respect. Their patriotism will be manifest by their witness to the world of America's openness to reason and truth, its acceptance of change, and its willingness to take the high road at all times.

Concluding remarks

All the statistics point to a fast-growing segment of our population that is "secular" — agnostic, atheist, whatever. A large part of them are young and many are unemployed, poor or just social misfits. Let us learn from history and do our best to get them involved in a "secular" setting, be it political, social, and so on. We know what will eventually happen in a vacuum. WE CANNOT ALLOW THEM TO LANGUISH IN A VACUUM! WE CANNOT ALLOW THEM TO BE SUCKED INTO RELIGIOUS, CRIMINAL, OR ANY OTHER KIND OF EXTREMISM. THE TIME HAS COME FOR SECULAR LEADERS TO EMERGE IN THIS COUNTRY AND HARNESS THE ENORMOUS POTENTIAL OUT THERE OR FACE THE TERRIBLE DEBACLE THAT WILL ENSUE.

I have spoken at great length about the truth that there is no personal God. It follows that religion is not truth. So what is left for us atheists to believe in, to reach for, to motivate us? Is it justice for all, universal peace, elimination of poverty, well-being for all, equal opportunity and so on? Why yes, it is all those things, and they are found in our daily lives, in politics, business, social interactions. Nothing has changed. It's just that it's time to step forward and take charge of our destiny. We have got to start pushing back on any and all religious influence on our politics and actions, approving them only when they have passed a purely secular evaluation using nothing but reason to guide us, and denouncing them otherwise. We could start by participating more fully in our democracy, hence my obsession with our electoral system.

The above may seem quixotic and chimerical, but believe me when I say that democracy needs constant vigilance. It is not a license to ridicule others, nor is it a license to impose one's way of life on a minority, nor is it about one-size-fits-all, to borrow from Arundhati Roy, or one style for all seasons. It is more like a plant that needs careful tending based on changing conditions, or it will wither and die. It is, simply put, like the Buddhism I talked about earlier — live and let live but do no harm to others. Churchill once said in a speech to the House of Commons "*Democracy is the worst form of government, except for all those other forms that have been tried from time to time.*" This implies that Democracy has imperfections and ours does too, so let us at least try to right the obvious imperfections we know about! Our Founding Fathers gave us a precious gift It is up to us to make sure it endures and prospers. By the way, when they crafted our nation two hundred and forty years ago it must have seemed as pie in the sky as do some of the above postulates.

What more is there to be said? We are confident that we will eventually prevail and sanity will return to this world. But how bad will it get before this happens? How much longer must *Homo sapiens* put up with his own creations—GOD and RELIGION—getting in the way? How committed must we all be? How best to once and for all dismantle the whole wretched mess? Should we start by once more harnessing those redemptive cooperation genes that more than seventy thousand years ago helped to firmly establish *H. sapiens* as a winner, to reach out to the disenchanted and segregated ethnic and religious minorities in our midst and welcome them into modern, truly pluralistic, and just societies, or should we rely on military might alone? By COOPERATION and projectiles is how our species survived, and by sticking with obsolete projectiles alone is probably how our hominid cousin species perished. History must guide us, but history must also make us do better, a lot better, than the 150 years or more it has taken to not quite eliminate racial prejudice from our midst here at home. We do not have that time to deal with ISIS or global warming, for that matter!

I turn to man, not God, and pray, "Please, for heaven's sake, get with it and SAVE THE PLANET FOR OUR HEIRS!"

July 2015

INDEX

H

I

J

M

P

R

S

T

U

ABOUT THE AUTHOR

Zbigniew Alexander was born and raised a devout Catholic, graduated with a Bachelor's degree in science and has lived and worked in four countries spanning three continents. He is now retired and lives in the Southeastern United States.

Mr. Alexander believes in the adage "in Rome do as the Romans do" and as a result, he is quite familiar with the major religions of the world—Christianity, Islam, Hinduism, Buddhism and Judaism. People the world over, he feels, are really alike, despite how deeply we each hold our distinct religious beliefs and customs.

Mr. Alexander became an atheist in his sixties and has come to believe that religion is a major irritant in global affairs. If the personal God that religion postulates does not exist, it is time to deconstruct our religions and construct a society that will better survive the new technological millennium.

The human race is well into the new Anthropocene era, of its own creation, and fraught with challenges it has never faced before. Steven Hawking recently intimated that this century will be crucial in terms of preparing for and facing those challenges. If we are to survive, the last thing we need is conflicting superstitions to muddy the waters.

CPSIA information can be obtained at www.ICGtesting.com
Printed in the USA
BVOW08s1232080416

443518BV00001B/88/P

9 781682 894385